Seaman Asahel Knapp

The Present Status of Rice Culture in the United States

Seaman Asahel Knapp

The Present Status of Rice Culture in the United States

ISBN/EAN: 9783744670227

Printed in Europe, USA, Canada, Australia, Japan

Cover: Foto ©ninafisch / pixelio.de

More available books at **www.hansebooks.com**

THE PRESENT STATUS

OF

RICE CULTURE IN THE UNITED STATES.

BY

S. A. KNAPP.

WASHINGTON:
GOVERNMENT PRINTING OFFICE.
1899.

BULLETIN No. 22.

U. S. DEPARTMENT OF AGRICULTURE.

DIVISION OF BOTANY.

THE PRESENT STATUS

OF

RICE CULTURE IN THE UNITED STATES.

BY

S. A. KNAPP.

WASHINGTON:
GOVERNMENT PRINTING OFFICE.
1899.

LETTER OF TRANSMITTAL.

U. S. Department of Agriculture,
Division of Botany,
Washington, D. C., October 13, 1899.

Sir: In the year 1898 the United States used 190,285,315 pounds of imported rice, in addition to the home-grown crop of 116,401,760 pounds. Of the common cereals, barley, maize, oats, rye, and wheat, the United States produced during the same period, in addition to the domestic consumption, an export quantity of 24,205,469,356 pounds. In the case of one cereal, rice, we produce only about half the amount we consume. Of all the others we produce an enormous surplus for export. This anomalous condition is due to the fact that rice, in addition to its tropical or subtropical character, is a crop grown chiefly on wet lands, where it has hitherto been impossible to use harvesting machinery. The crop must therefore be cut with a sickle, and American hand labor has been thrown into competition with the cheap labor of the Tropics, a competition that has not proved profitable to the American. Under dry-land cultivation rice is a precarious crop. From all these circumstances rice cultivation in the United States has not attained in past years the full development of a prosperous industry.

In 1880 a peculiar prairie region extending along the coast of southwestern Louisiana was opened up by the construction of a railroad. In 1884 enterprising settlers began the development of a new system of rice culture, by which, as now perfected, the elevated and normally or periodically dry prairie lands are flooded by a system of pumps, canals, and levees, and when the rice is about to mature the water is drained off, leaving the land dry enough for the use of reaping machines. Under this system the cost of harvesting, and therefore the total cost of production, have been greatly reduced and the industry has undergone a rapid development. In 1896 the depressing effects of a new difficulty began to be heavily felt. The varieties of rice most productive and otherwise satisfactory from a cultural standpoint under the new system were defective commercially, because the percentage of grains broken in the process of milling or preparing the grain for market was very large, and the proportion of "head rice," made up of unbroken grains, was low. The difference in wholesale price between head rice and broken rice is about 2 cents per pound. When the broken rice ran up to 40, 60, or even 90 per cent, and in the face of a close market, the whole industry was menaced.

3

On the 1st of July, 1898, an appropriation for the introduction of valuable seeds and plants from foreign countries, asked for by the Secretary of Agriculture in his estimates of the preceding year, became available, and on September 1, 1898, Dr. S. A. Knapp, of Louisiana, was appointed by the Secretary as an agricultural explorer, with instructions to visit Japan, investigate the rices of that country, and purchase a stock suited to meet the requirements of the American problem. Dr. Knapp returned in the early spring of 1899 with 10 tons of Kiushu rice, which was distributed to experimenters in southwestern Louisiana and elsewhere in the rice belt. The result of the milling tests are now awaited. If the high milling quality of the Kiushu rice is maintained under our cultural conditions, the last apparent obstacle to the complete success of an American system of rice cultivation will be removed.

The accompanying report by Dr. Knapp, entitled The Present Status of Rice Culture in the United States, has been prepared for the purpose of diffusing information on the new American system of rice culture and its relation to the general question of rice production. I recommend its publication as Bulletin No. 22 of this Division.

Respectfully,

FREDERICK V. COVILLE,
Botanist.

Hon. JAMES WILSON,
Secretary of Agriculture.

CONTENTS.

ILLUSTRATIONS.

THE PRESENT STATUS OF RICE CULTURE IN THE UNITED STATES.

INTRODUCTORY.

Rice forms the principal food of one-half the population of the earth. It is never the exclusive food of a people except under necessity for short periods, but it has just claims to a wider and more general use as a food material than any other cereal.

Where dense populations are dependent for food upon an annual crop and any considerable diminution in the supply would result in starvation for many, rice has been selected as the staple food wherever the climate permits its cultivation. Among dense populations certainty of supply is of first importance.

The luxuriant growth of leguminous plants at all seasons in tropical climates provides the necessary nitrogenous food elements. Nitrogenous foods are more economically provided in this way than in the form of meats as used by the European races.

A combination of rice and pulses is a much cheaper complete food than wheat and meat, and forms a food ration which may be produced on a smaller tilled area. The individual workers in densely populated agricultural countries are forced to depend on the cheapest suitable rations; hence, the popular dependence on rice and legumes in such closely-settled lands as Japan, China, and India.

The estimated population of the Chinese Empire is 402,000,000; of the British possessions in Asia, 291,000,000; of Japan, 43,000,000; and of other rice-eating countries, 90,000,000. It is estimated that rice constitutes fully half of the entire food supply of these nations.

North and South America, Europe, and Australia are not included among the rice-eating nations, though the people of these countries consume considerable quantities.

ORIGIN AND HISTORY.

Rice cultivation is older than authentic history; it is associated with the traditions and mythology of primeval nations. The rice plant was undoubtedly a native of southeastern Asia from Madras to Cochin China, but was first cultivated by the Chinese. It was known to the early Greeks and Romans and had spread throughout the tropics before the commencement of the Christian era.

VARIETIES OF RICE.

There is an immense number of varieties of cultivated rice, differing in length of the season required for maturing, and in character, yield, and quality. Their divergence not only extends to size, shape, and color of the grain, but to the relative proportion of food constituents and the

7

consequent flavor. South Carolina and Japan rices are rich in fats, and hence are ranked in flavor and nutrition among rice-eating nations as much above Patna, which is very poor in fats, as well-fattened beef is esteemed superior to the lean animals of the range. A botanical catalogue enumerates 161 varieties found in Ceylon alone, while in Japan, China, and India, where its cultivation has gone on for centuries, and where great care is usually taken in the improvement of the crop by the selection of seed, no less than 1,400 varieties are said to exist.

RICE IN THE UNITED STATES.

MANNER OF INTRODUCTION.

An account which appears to be authentic says that rice was grown in Virginia by Sir William Berkley as early as 1647. No particulars are given, except that from a half a bushel of seed planted the product was 16 bushels. Governor Alston, of South Carolina, in an agricultural address (1854) says: "Rice, for which we are indebted to the island of Madagascar, was introduced into Carolina toward the close of the seventeenth century (1694)." Governor Alston states that a few seeds of this Madagascar rice were sown in a garden which is now one of the thickly-built portions of Charleston, and from that seed came the rice that has made South Carolina famous as a rice-producing State. Ramsay's History of South Carolina states that an English or Dutch ship, homeward bound from Madagascar, was driven by stress of weather to seek shelter in the harbor of Charleston, and the captain seized the opportunity to visit an old acquaintance, the landgrave and governor of the province, Thomas Smith, whom he had already met in Madagascar. Smith expressed the desire to experiment with the growing of rice upon a low, moist patch of ground in his garden, similar to the ground upon which he had seen rice growing in Madagascar, whereupon the captain presented him with a small bag of rice seed which happened to be among the ship's stores. The seed was planted in a garden in Longitude lane, Charleston, the spot being still pointed out.

PRODUCTION AND IMPORTATION.

Rice-growing sections.—Rice production in the United States is limited to the South Atlantic and Gulf States, where, in some sections, it is the principal cereal product. For nearly one hundred and ninety years after the introduction of rice into the United States, South Carolina and Georgia produced the principal portion, while North Carolina, Florida, Alabama, Mississippi, and Louisiana grew only a limited amount. Within the last ten years Louisiana and Texas have increased the area devoted to rice to such an extent that they now furnish three-fourths of all the product of the country. In 1896 Louisiana produced 127,600,000 pounds of rice, North and South Carolina 27,901,440 pounds, and Georgia 10,464,000 pounds.

Production.—The present annual production of rice in the United States is considerably less than the consumption. The total product from 1892 to 1896, inclusive, was 898,563,900 pounds, and the total amount imported during the same period 794,563,900 pounds.

The following estimates of the rice produced in the principal rice-growing States are considerably below the actual product, as they represent only the amounts placed upon the market. The quantities consumed at home and retained for seed are considerable, but can not well be determined.

Marketed production of rice in the United States from 1847 to 1898.

[Statistics Dan Talmage's Sons Co. Pounds cleaned. Figures each year for crop of preceding year.]

Year.	North and South Carolina.	Georgia.	Louisiana.	Total.
1847	93,488,800	22,043,400		115,477,200
1848	81,381,000	21,081,600		102,462,600
1849	96,751,200	22,408,800		119,160,000
1850	86,662,600	25,675,200		112,237,800
1851	81,414,600	21,361,200		102,775,800
1852	81,776,400	23,957,400		105,733,800
1853	84,188,400	18,279,000		102,467,400
1854	82,981,800	18,448,800		101,430,600
1855	64,150,200	6,721,866		70,872,000
1856	85,662,000	17,944,200		103,606,200
1857	83,043,000	16,521,600		99,664,600
1858	89,436,600	18,807,000		108,243,600
1859	93,667,800	22,625,400		116,293,200
1860	96,516,000	21,369,000		117,885,000
1861	82,171,200	21,429,000	1,679,000	106,279,200
1862	(1)	(1)	2,051,830	2,051,830
1863	(1)	(1)	2,086,280	2,086,280
1864	(1)	(1)	1,580,790	1,580,790
1865	2,471,400	(1)	2,269,180	4,740,580
1866	7,500,000	(1)	2,746,490	10,246,490
1867	12,018,600	8,429,200	4,706,720	25,154,720
1868	16,659,600	6,171,800	4,982,590	27,813,790
1869	23,428,200	10,720,800	9,502,910	43,651,910
1870	25,423,200	15,217,800	13,329,880	53,970,880
1871	25,800,000	15,000,000	14,088,880	54,888,880
1872	25,705,200	[2]6,750,000	[2]6,870,790	39,325,990
1873	28,344,000	11,924,400	12,007,380	52,275,780
1874	25,840,200	14,221,200	22,338,980	62,400,380
1875	28,360,800	13,002,600	26,450,000	67,813,400
1876	27,354,500	15,106,200	41,400,000	83,860,800
1877	28,940,400	16,087,800	41,630,000	86,628,200
1878	26,926,200	17,914,200	[2]32,892,000	77,732,400
1879	25,304,400	18,437,400	[2]37,772,000	81,513,800
1880	[3]38,252,400	24,344,400	25,000,000	85,596,800

Year.	North Carolina.	South Carolina.	Georgia.	Louisiana.	Total.
1881	5,160,000	30,052,200	24,715,200	51,941,590	111,868,990
1882	8,220,000	[2]20,815,200	[2]18,345,000	55,224,610	102,604,810
1883	7,128,000	[2]27,349,800	[2]18,457,200	47,150,000	99,995,000
1884	7,487,600	26,913,000	21,119,400	55,200,000	110,700,000
1885	8,292,900	32,366,700	22,902,000	46,000,000	109,561,600
1886	[2]5,250,000	30,398,700	[2]14,496,300	100,050,000	150,195,000
1887	9,000,000	32,395,800	19,973,700	94,300,000	155,669,500
1888	5,400,000	28,455,000	11,975,700	67,800,000	113,630,700
1889	6,131,500	26,637,300	13,709,400	81,250,000	124,733,200
1890	6,818,700	30,432,900	15,095,400	79,375,000	131,722,000
1891	7,650,400	28,275,000	13,125,000	87,750,000	136,800,000
1892	6,697,800	27,182,900	12,005,700	109,778,200	155,665,600
1893	6,818,400	33,250,500	15,078,000	182,400,000	237,546,900
1894	[2]3,937,500	[2]11,372,445	[2]8,688,015	[3]98,867,200	122,865,160
1895	4,000,000	22,354,800	[2]6,656,000	[3]76,800,000	109,820,800
1896	2,720,000	27,901,440	10,464,000	[4]127,600,000	168,605,440
1897	2,720,000	29,532,160	[2]8,727,040	[3]55,907,200	96,846,400
1898	2,080,000	28,395,200	10,181,760	[3][5]75,644,800	116,301,760
1899	2,560,000	23,054,720	3,584,000	107,792,000	136,990,720

[1] No report for North and South Carolina or Georgia—civil war.　　　[2] Harvest storms.
[3] Drought during growing season in Louisiana.
[4] Unfavorable growing conditions. Large per cent of poor quality, and, because of exceptionally low values, devoted to feeding purposes; not reaching commercial channels.
[5] Reduced acreage.

The average annual production, or rather the amount annually marketed, during the ten years from 1887 to 1896 was about 145,120,000 pounds of cleaned rice. The maximum crop during that period was 237,546,000 pounds, in 1893, while the lowest was 109,820,000 pounds, in 1895. The annual production for the eleven years immediately preceding the civil war ranged from 70,872,000 pounds, in 1855, to 117,885,000, in 1860, and averaged about 100,000,000 pounds.

Imports.—The following table shows the amounts of rice and rice products imported into the United States during the fiscal years[1] from 1894 to 1899:

Imports of rice into the United States.

Year ended June 30—	Rice.		Rice—flour, meal, and broken.		Total.	
	Pounds.	Value.	Pounds.	Value.	Pounds.	Value.
1894	86,810,536	$1,540,992	55,351,281	$833,843	142,161,820	$2,374,835
1895	141,301,411	2,353,974	78,262,909	1,091,538	219,564,320	3,445,512
1896	78,190,373	1,274,574	68,534,273	911,005	146,724,646	2,185,579
1897	133,939,930	2,555,960	63,876,204	961,200	197,816,134	3,517,160
1898	129,810,630	2,793,111	60,474,685	953,722	190,285,315	3,746,833
1899	153,837,026	3,152,771	50,340,267	777,378	204,177,293	3,930,149

As will be seen from this table the annual imports of rice for the six years averaged more than 120,000,000 pounds, while that of broken rice, flour, and meal averaged 62,000,000 pounds. From this it would appear that there is room for a two-thirds increase in the total production before the home markets will be supplied by home-grown rice.

Tariff.—The present duty on rice is as follows:

Cents.

Cleaned rice, per pound 2

Uncleaned (hull removed, cuticle on) 1¼

Paddy .... ⅞

Broken rice (very fine, passing through No. 12 sieve) .... ¼

Rice flour, rice meal .... ¼

CAN THE UNITED STATES GROW ITS OWN RICE?

Rice is a plant of such vigor that it could be grown on any arable land as far north as the Ohio River but for three reasons:

CONDITIONS OF PRODUCTION.

Irrigation.—The crop must be irrigated. The smaller tributaries of the rivers that drain the Mississippi Valley bring down very little water during the summer. The same is true of the smaller creeks and streams emptying directly into the Gulf. The flood period, or the time of the year when there is the greatest abundance of water, is not coincident with the period during which the largest amount of water is required by the rice crop. In the absence of lakes or natural reservoirs throughout this region it would be necessary to raise the water

---

[1] The fiscal year ends June 30.

from the streams by pumping, and it is an open question whether the water supply would be large enough for any extended area of rice lands.

Moist climate.—Rice, to attain its best development, also requires a moist climate. With irrigation alone rice would mature among the mountains of Tennessee, but the crop would not compare in quality or quantity with the crops grown along the Gulf and Atlantic coasts, and hence could not compete with the latter in the world's markets. As an example, in southwestern Louisiana the winds from the Gulf are laden with moisture, but the north winds are dry, and consequently the lands along the south side of a lake or large pond usually produce 2 barrels per acre more than on the north side, although other conditions of soil and moisture may be equal. Again, the Island of Kiushu, Japan, produces on an average 3 barrels of rice per acre more than the remainder of the Empire. This is because the island is situated where the warm ocean currents first strike the cooler lands and give off a large amount of moisture.

Soil conditions.—The best rice lands are underlaid by an impervious subsoil. Otherwise the land can not be satisfactorily drained at time of harvest in order to permit the use of improved harvesting machinery. The alluvial lands along the Mississippi Valley in Louisiana are not underlaid by hardpan, and they can not be drained sufficiently to permit the use of heavy harvesters and teams of horses.

AREA OF LANDS SUITABLE FOR RICE CULTURE.

According to the best estimates there are about 10,000,000 acres of land in the five States bordering the Gulf of Mexico well suited to rice cultivation. The amount which can be successfully irrigated by present methods, using the available surface and artesian flows, does not exceed 3,000,000 acres. The balance of the land could probably be brought into cultivation were it necessary, but the cost would, perhaps, be prohibitive at present prices. Three million acres is a conservative estimate of the amount which can be successfully irrigated. The best results require rotation of crops; consequently only one-half of that amount, or 1,500,000 acres, would be in rice at any one time. At an average yield of 10 barrels (of 162 pounds) per acre, 1,500,000 acres of rice would produce nearly 2,500,000,000 pounds of cleaned rice, nearly six times the amount of our present consumption. It will be noted by referring to the preceding table (p. 10) that the imports for 1899 show a considerable increase over preceding years. The crop harvested in 1899 is said to be the largest which has ever been grown. Unofficial estimates place it at 300,000,000 pounds. It would appear from these figures that the demand for rice and rice products is increasing in the United States.

PROSPECTS FOR EXTENSION OF RICE INDUSTRY.

The outlook for the further extension of the industry is very promising. There has been recently quite an awakening among the farmers to the importance of this industry, so that there have been large annual increases in the area planted. There is no satisfactory reason why the United States should not grow and mill all of its own rice, nor is there any reason why the United States should not become an exporter.

The Gold Seed South Carolina rice sells for as much as any rice in the markets. The ordinary lowland rices are much better in quality than the ordinary (non-irrigated) upland rices, provided they are grown on soils which can be drained, but there is a great difference in different varieties, especially in the hardness of the grain. The most desirable rice from the standpoint of the grower is one which will produce the largest amount of "head rice," that is, unbroken grains. Upland rices, or lowland rices of poor quality, break up during the process of milling, so that the percentage of head rice often averages only 40, or 30, or sometimes even as low as 10 per cent of the entire crop. The Japanese rices average better than the American as far as their milling qualities are concerned, and for this reason it is desirable that Japanese rices be more extensively introduced into this country, provided they maintain here the same characteristics as in their native country. The Department of Agriculture has recently imported a small amount (about 10 tons) of high-grade rice from Japan.

There is the further consideration that, as will be explained below, the adoption of the use of machinery in the rice fields similar to that used in the great wheat fields of California and the Dakotas is resulting in a revolution in methods of cultivation, greatly reducing the cost. The American rice grower, employing higher-priced labor than any other rice grower of the world, will ultimately be able to market his crop at the least cost and the greatest profit. If, in addition, the same relative improvement can be secured in the rice itself; if varieties which yield from 80 to 90 per cent of head rice in the finished product can be successfully introduced, American rice growers will be able to command the highest prices for their product in the markets of the world.

METHODS OF RICE CULTIVATION IN THE UNITED STATES.

The different rice-growing sections of the South use different methods of irrigation, seeding, cultivation, harvesting, and curing. A comprehensive report on the general subject of rice cultivation may be best made by treating each of these sections or regions separately, thus emphasizing points of difference or similarity.

SOUTH CAROLINA AND GEORGIA.

The preeminence in rice cultivation in the United States which South Carolina has enjoyed for two hundred years has been won by careful attention to the selection of seed and by thorough cultivation.

EFFECT OF CIVIL WAR ON RICE INDUSTRY.

Rice culture in South Carolina and Georgia had so developed through a long series of years that delta lands, improved and ready for rice cultivation, were worth, prior to 1860, from $200 to $300 per acre, and were considered among the most profitable investments for capital. From 1861 to 1866 most of these lands were uncultivated and in many instances the improvements were destroyed. This, with the high price of labor since 1866, has reduced the value of the lands to less than the cost of improvements; in some cases to $25 or $30 per acre. Prominent planters, in speaking of the condition of the rice industry at the close of the war, describe the situation in the following terms:

The industry had been remanded to its infancy. The planters had returned to their estates to find buildings, machinery, and implements destroyed; the appliances of a wonderful system of irrigation and drainage mutilated or wrecked; the long-abandoned fields grown up in tangled wilds of brush, vines, and trees; the once disciplined and supremely efficient labor of the country turned into a mob. It should be no marvel that the great majority of the planters recoiled from an industry which seemed only a desperate adventure. A few who undertook the work of recuperation succeeded at the risk of the little capital or credit left to them and often at the peril of life itself. Many failed; none so wretchedly as those who were unfamiliar with a culture demanding peculiar experience and skill, or who were unable to adapt themselves successfully to the new régime of labor and to the unexpected character of employees who had yet to learn the severe lesson of quickly earned and untried liberty. In short, relegated to its earliest historical conditions, the rice industry of the South was practically commenced anew, and, if it had any encouragement at all, it was in the protection afforded by the import tax on foreign rice. The crops were cultivated for many years at extraordinary cost and at great hazard. The embarrassments were diminished in process of time, and meanwhile, as labor became more efficient and less costly and the consumption of rice increased, so the area of cultivation and production expanded.

VARIETIES GROWN.

The gold-seed rice, justly famous for the quality and large yield of the grain, stands, in the estimation of the market, among the first rices in the world. Along the Atlantic coast it has practically superseded the white rice introduced and generally cultivated in the earlier periods of the industry. The two varieties of gold-seed appear to differ little except that one variety has a slightly larger grain than the other. White rice is valued for its early maturity. The accompanying table illustrates the difference between the grains of gold-seed rice and white rice:

	Length of the grain.	Circumference around shorter axis.	Number of grains in one Troy ounce.
	Inches.	Inches.	
Gold seed, long grain	0.417	0.375	841
Gold seed, short grain	0.375	0.375	896
White rice	0.375	0.375	960

DELTA LANDS.

A large proportion of the rice grown in South Carolina and Georgia is produced on tidal deltas. A body of land along some river and sufficiently remote from the sea to be free from salt water is selected with reference to the possibility of flooding it from the river at high tide and of draining it at low tide.

Canals and levees.—A canal is excavated on the outer rim of this tract, completely inclosing the field. The excavated dirt is thrown upon the outer bank. The canal must be of sufficient capacity for irrigation and drainage, and must also furnish dirt to make a levee which will provide perfect protection against the encroachments of the river at all seasons. The tract is then cut up by smaller canals into fields of 10 to 12 acres, making small levees on the border of each field. The fields are subdivided by ditches into strips 20 or 30 feet wide for cultivation. The entire tract is usually nearly level, but if there should be any inequality care must be taken that the surface of each subfield be level. The main canal is 10 to 30 feet wide and about 4 feet deep, and connects with the river by flood gates. Through these canals boats of considerable tonnage have ready access to the entire circuit of the tract, while smaller boats can pass along the subcanals to the several fields. The subcanals are usually from 6 to 10 feet in width and should be nearly as deep as the main canal.

Drainage.—Perfect drainage is one of the most important considerations in rice farming, because upon it depends the proper condition of the soil for planting. It may appear unimportant that a water plant like rice should have aerated and finely pulverized soil for the seed bed, but such is the case. Thorough cultivation seems to be as beneficial to rice as to wheat. Complete and rapid drainage at harvest always insures the saving of the crop under the best conditions and reduces the expense of the harvest. On 500 acres of such land, well prepared, there should be 65 to 80 miles of ditches, canals, and embankment.

If there are logs, stumps, or stones in the field they must be removed. When practicable the rice lands are flooded from the river and find drainage by a canal or subsidiary stream that enters the river at a lower level. The embankment must be sufficient to protect the rice against either freshets or salt water. Freshets are injurious to growing rice, not only because of the volume of water but by reason of the temperature. A great body of water descending rapidly from the mountains to the sea is several degrees colder than water under the ordinary flow. Any large amount of this cold water admitted to the field, not only retards the growth but is a positive injury to the crop. In periods of continued drought the salt water of the sea frequently ascends the river a considerable distance. Slightly brackish water is not injurious to rice, but salt water is destructive.

INLAND MARSHES.

Some excellent marshes are found in South Carolina and Georgia upon what may relatively be termed high land. These are in most cases easily drained and in many instances can be irrigated from some convenient stream. The objection planters have found to such tracts is that the water supply is unreliable and not uniform in temperature. In case of drought the supply may be insufficient; in case of freshets the water is too cold. To obviate these objections reservoirs are some-times constructed, but are expensive, owing to loss by the evaporation from such a large exposed surface. However, where all the conditions are favorable, it costs less to improve these upland marshes than the delta lands and the results are fairly remunerative.

CULTIVATION.

During the flooding period the ditches and canals become more or less filled by the mud which flows into them with the water. As soon after harvest as possible the ditch banks are cleared of foul grasses, weeds, or brush, and the ditches are cleaned. The levees are exam-ined to see if they are in repair. Early in the winter the fields are plowed or dug over with a heavy hoe. At this time the plowing is shallow, about 4 inches deep. The field is then barely covered with water, which later is drained off. Upon this saturated soil the frost acts with considerable force, disintegrating it and pulverizing the lumps. In March the land is allowed to dry, all the drains being placed in repair and kept open. Seeding commences in April and con-tinues nearly to the middle of May. Just prior to seeding the land is thoroughly harrowed, all clods pulverized and the surface smoothed. Trenches 12 inches apart and 2 to 3 inches deep are made with 4-inch trenching hoes at right angles to the drains, and the seed is dropped in these at the rate of 114 to 135 pounds to the acre. Great attention is paid to the selection of good seed. This is usually covered, but occasionally a planter, to save labor, stirs the seed in clayed water, enough clay adhering to the kernels to prevent their floating away when the water is admitted. Under the usual method the water is let on as soon as the seed is covered, and remains on four to six days, till the grain is well sprouted. It is then withdrawn. As soon as the blade is up a few inches the water is sometimes put on for a few days and again withdrawn. The first water is locally called the "sprout water." After the rice has two leaves the so-called "stretch water" or "long point flow" is put on. At first it is allowed to be deep enough to cover the rice completely—generally from 10 to 12 inches—then it is gradually drawn down to about 6 inches, where it is held twenty to thirty days. It is then withdrawn and the field allowed to dry. When the field is sufficiently dry the rice is hoed thoroughly, all grass and "volunteer" rice being carefully removed. After hoeing it remains without irrigation until jointing commences, when it is slightly hoed, care being used to prevent injury to the plant, and the water is then turned on to the field. During the time water is held on the rice it is changed at least every week to avoid its becoming stagnant. When this occurs rice is liable to be troubled with the water weevil. This "lay-by flow," or final irrigation, continues until about eight days before the harvest, when the water is drawn off for the field to dry.

Farmers differ considerably in their methods; some hoe more than twice and some flood more than three times, and some less; also in the final flooding the practices differ as to the depth of water maintained; some farmers consider it advantageous to keep the water nearly as deep as the rice stem is tall till shortly before harvest and then gradually withdraw the water as the straw stiffens; others prefer only sufficient water to properly mature the crop. The Hon. John Screven, of Savannah, Ga., an eminent authority on rice, states that irrigation along the northern rivers of South Carolina and even as far south as Charleston differs from that pursued around Savannah in Georgia, owing to the fact that the former lands are generally low and can be plowed or flooded at any time, which is not usually the case with the Georgia land. The time the water is held on the field in the "long point flow," he claims, should depend upon the condition of the crop, and every planter must decide that for himself. He must observe the plant and allow it to acquire proper root support before making any radical change. In regard to the "harvest water," he says:

On the start the depth should correspond to the "long point water" and should be increased with the growth of the plant, but should never rise above the collar of the leaf. This flow should be put on when, on clearing the base of the stalk of the plant, an open joint is shown. This is the initial of the grain formation and should be aided by the water.

YIELD AND VALUE OF PRODUCT PER ACRE.

Good delta lands are estimated to yield, under intelligent management, from 30 to 45 bushels to the acre. The standard weight of rough rice in commerce is 45 pounds to the bushel. In a report made by planters to the Savannah Rice Association, January 28, 1882, the average yield to the acre is placed at 30 bushels, and the annual cost of cultivation, including interest on the land, at $35 per acre. In a report made by prominent rice planters to the House Committee on Ways and Means in January, 1897, the average yield to the acre is placed at 32 bushels, and the cost of production is fixed at $24. If we take the latter estimate the cost to the planter in the Atlantic States of raising 100 pounds of rough rice is $1.66, or $2.69 per sack of 162 pounds. Of course this is only an average, the cost being much less in some instances and in others much greater.

NORTH CAROLINA, FLORIDA, AND MISSISSIPPI.

Considerable rice is produced in these States, but as the methods are similar to those practiced in South Carolina and Georgia it is unnecessary to describe them here. In these States there are quite large tracts which could profitably be devoted to rice and which are almost useless for other purposes. With the denser population of ensuing years these now waste lands will be improved and become valuable accessories to their wealth. In many sections of Florida a little capital judiciously invested in the improvement of rice lands would bring profitable returns. In southern Mississippi there are large tracts that could be purchased at nominal figures and devoted to rice.

EASTERN LOUISIANA.

For many years small fields of rice were planted in this State to add to the food supply, but commercially rice was scarcely considered by the planters until 1865, when they were confronted by the problem of how to utilize large and desolated sugar plantations without available resources. What was at first planted for a food supply proved to be a profitable crop and the rice industry made rapid strides. In 1864 the total rice crop of Louisiana was 1,580,790 pounds; in 1866 it was 4,706,720 pounds; in 1868, 9,509,910 pounds; in 1874, 22,338,980 pounds; and in 1877, 41,630,000 pounds. At first plantations were leased, in many instances, and planted a few years while they produced a maximum crop, when they were abandoned for other lands which had not hitherto been planted in rice. This change of lands was due to the rapid increase of harmful grasses, many of which were conveyed to the fields by the irrigating water, and appeared to find such congenial conditions for growth that in about three years they were practically in full possession. In a short time it became evident that the practical supply of plantations for such purposes was limited, and that the planters must learn both to keep their fields clean from grass and maintain their fertility.

RICE GROWING ON THE LOW LANDS.

The following letter from Hon. John Dymond, a prominent planter, and for many years president of the Louisiana State Agricultural Society, gives a succinct statement of the low-land cultivation south of New Orleans:

System of levees.—Rice on the Mississippi River has generally been raised on old sugar plantations, where the ditches run down the line of descent of the land, which was excellent so far as the drainage was concerned, but the ditch banks were of no service in flooding the lands. (Along the Mississippi River the banks are highest next the stream and generally descend toward the drainage in the rear.) For flooding the lands the so-called check levees were thrown across the line of fall of the land sufficiently near to each other so that any small levee not exceeding 2 feet in height could hold back water enough to reach up the incline until another check levee intervened. Where the lands had but little fall but few check levees were necessary, and where the fall was great there had to be many of them. I should say that ordinarily a check levee was required every 400 feet. As the sugar plantation ditches were hardly ever more than 200 feet apart and the check levees but from 200 to 400 feet apart, the result was very small fields of from 1 to 2 acres, in which machines could not be worked to advantage. Therefore the harvesting machines have never been used with much success on the river.

These check levees cross the old ditches with either plank or earthen dams, and the size of the plats of the land would vary from 1 to 2 acres up to 10 to 20 acres, if the water could be held on such a large space. I should say, however, that fields of this size were very rare in the river rice districts, little fields of 5 to 10 acres being far more numerous.

Flooding.—On the lower coast the fields are flooded before any work is done; they are plowed in the water; the rice is then sowed upon the fields and harrowed in the wet. The water is then taken off and the rice germinates at once. It has to be nursed very carefully with water for fear the young rice may be scalded by the hot sun, the planting not being done until late in April or in May. In what is generally known as dry culture the land is prepared as for oats and carefully harrowed. The rice is then planted broadcast or with drills—generally broadcast—and when it comes up, or rather after it comes up, the lands are moistened with water and the water kept a little below the tops of the plants, following them up as they grow taller. The water is not taken off these plants unless, as is commonly thought, they are attacked by crayfish. This, however, is regarded by many as doubtful. Sometimes an increased quantity is put upon the lands for the purpose of covering the plants so as to drown the caterpillars that attack them at this stage of growth. Flooding the land several times, as is practiced in South Carolina, is not known here. If no mishap occurs to the crop the water is kept upon it constantly from the time it comes above the ground until the lands are drained off preparatory to harvesting.

Preparing land and sowing seed.—For dry culture, the lands are plowed in winter. For wet culture, the lands are only plowed about the time of planting—say, in April. In dry culture it is considered good practice to sow late in March, and reasonably good practice to sow in April. In wet culture it is expedient to sow before the latter part of April. Rice planted up to the 15th of May is considered good for a fair yield; planted after that the yield will be cut down in quantity. If planted late in June it matures so late in the fall that the cold nights are apt to shrivel it and but a small crop will be realized. On the river the rice is generally sown by hand. Broadcast seeding machines have been used, but not to any extent. Some rice has been planted with drills, but they never obtained much use among the river planters.

Harvesting and thrashing.—The rice is cut when it matures, generally in August, and is put in shocks of about 20 bundles each. It ordinarily remains in these shocks about a week, during which time the shock dries out some and may heat a little. The old rice planters think it wise to then carry the rice into a yard called a battery, and to stack it there carefully, where it undergoes some sweating, during which it is liable to stack burn. Most of our river planters, however, now prefer to cut the rice, to tie it up, to ship it off after a few days only, and to haul directly from the shocks to the thrashing machine, the rice lying sufficiently long on the stubble to dry it before it is tied up, and very little curing is then required in the shocks. Practically all of the rice is thrashed at once; whereas, if stacked, it sometimes burns if left too damp. Under my own observation there has been produced on this land as high as 30 barrels (4,860 pounds) of rough rice per acre. This was upon good land that had been in peas and had been fall-plowed with six-mule teams. The average product per acre on the lower coast (Mississippi River) will not exceed 8 barrels, and 12 barrels is considered a good crop.

Wet culture and weeds.—I think the same general rules will apply to the upper coast, but usually on the upper coast they resort to dry culture, while the lowness of our rice lands on the lower coast leads to a great deal of plowing actually in the water. Again, our people plow in the water, because what are called our best rice lands are buckshot clay, and they are so stiff that the average small rice planter can not plow them with any team that he has, unless he softens them up in this way. Wet culture is a very delicate process and unless done just right is apt to end disastrously, whereas with dry culture the rice crop will come up as certainly as an oat crop, with the danger, however, of a large growth of grass coming along with it. Our planters become very skillful with their wet culture, and always strive to get rice up ahead of the grasses, but still the lowness of our lands gives a constant supply of injurious grasses and weeds that have to be picked out by hand. For this reason I have always thought that the rice lands in the western part of the State were bound to supply the whole consumption of the country, owing to the facts that they could be readily drained, that our lowland weeds do not prevail there, and that the culture was rendered incomparably cheaper by the use of harvesting machines.

RICE GROWING ON WELL-DRAINED ALLUVIAL LANDS.

On the well-drained alluvial lands above New Orleans, the fields are ditched and leveed as described in the foregoing account of the lower coast rice growing. Particular attention is given to thorough drainage in February, and by the first of March the land should be ready for the plow. The land should be well plowed and harrowed. Some advocate shallow plowing and some claim that deep plowing is better. Conditions vary so widely that no absolute rule will apply, but where the water supply is ample a depth of 6 inches will be found fairly satisfactory. Sowing is generally done broadcast and by hand, at the rate of 50 to 80 pounds to the acre, and followed by a thorough harrowing of the land. Sowing generally commences about the 20th of March, and is completed by the middle of April, the object being to place the rice upon the market as early as possible, before the price is affected by the foreign crop or that of southwestern Louisiana and Texas.

Sowing the seed.—Three different methods of treating the seed are followed. Some let on just enough water to saturate the ground immediately after sowing and harrowing and at once draw off any surplus water. This insures the germination of the seed. Others sow and trust to there being sufficient moisture in the land to germinate the seed. This is sometimes uncertain, and rarely produces the best results. A few sprout the seed before planting by placing bags of rice in water. This is sure to be a failure if the soil is very dry when the seed is sown. In case of planting in dry soil, without following with water saturation, rolling the land after seeding and harrowing has been found beneficial.

Flooding.—When the young rice is 5 or 6 inches high, water is generally let on to the field, care being exercised that it should not entirely cover the plants, and the field is kept continuously submerged until the crop matures. Where the soil is sufficiently moist to promote growth, some of the planters do not turn on the water until the rice is 10 inches high. It is claimed by them that there is great danger of sun-scalding if water is allowed on the field when the rice is very young and tender.

As soon as the rice stalks indicate any change in color at the bottom the water is turned off.

Harvesting.—Formerly the rice was cut, allowed to dry one day, and then bound and placed in small shocks for further curing. It usually remained in the shock a week, and was then stacked. The stack was round, not more than 6 or 8 feet in diameter, and built upon a plank base about 2 feet from the ground. Recently many planters pursue the methods of cutting, curing, and threshing described by Mr. Dymond. It is not practicable, on this class of lands, to employ machinery in cutting the rice.

OBSTACLES ENCOUNTERED.

Expense of flooding.—The water used in flooding the alluvial lands along the Mississippi River was formerly drawn from the river by a pipe which pierced the base of the levee. These pipes were a constant menace to security from freshets. A majority of the disastrous breaks in the levees were attributable to them. Finally the law prohibited their further use and required that the water be drawn over the levee, which considerably increased the cost of obtaining water for flooding.

Weedy grasses.—In all delta rice lands the rapid increase of injurious grasses becomes a serious question. This is intensified along the Mississippi by the large amount and wonderful variety of grass seed in the river water. The question of disposing of these grasses was fully treated by H. S. Wilkinson in a paper before the Jefferson Parish (La.) Agricultural Society. He made the following suggestions:

While the attempts to get rid of grass have only scored failures, there is no doubt that grasses can be thinned out considerably. From the varieties we have to contend with, embracing as they do seeds that germinate from February to June, it is hardly possible, under the present methods, to destroy them entirely. The chief source of supply for these grass seeds is the suckers that shoot out from the old stalks which are cut with the rice. In fifteen days after the field is cut these suckers, which grow with wonderful rapidity, are "in seed" again.

Mowing and burning the grasses.—I have met with some success in destroying this supply by following up the harvester with a mowing machine, cutting everything down, allowing it to dry, and then burning it. To do this enough time must elapse before the mowing machine is started to allow the suckers to send out new leaves, so that when cut there will be enough straw on the ground to burn. Mowing without burning is almost useless. The fire is what does the work, destroying not only the seed but the root itself, thus effectually preventing any further suckerings. Any seeds that are left by the fire are exposed, will germinate during the first warm wet spell, and will be destroyed by the first frost. A great objection to this plan is that it leaves the land perfectly bare, to be impoverished by the parching August and September sun, and baking it so hard that it is difficult to plow. This objection would condemn it as a practical failure, and we have yet to find out some better plan of destroying this supply of seed before we can ever hope to succeed in establishing permanent rice plantations.

Winter flooding a failure.—If these grass seeds are not destroyed in the fall, they are scattered broadcast by the wind, protected from heat and cold by the luxurious growth, and only germinate when the continuous warmth of spring, penetrating the ground, causes all vegetation to start. I thought these seeds might be destroyed in winter by keeping them under water, and, on one occasion, having a place well located for that purpose, I kept a field under water all winter, and had it plowed in the spring. The straw, and, in fact, all vegetable matter had rotted, leaving the land perfectly clean, but a few days of exposure to the sun brought out a first-class stand of grass. The grass seeds will not rot without germinating, and they will not germinate in cold water.

The best plan of dealing with grass.—Having thus seen that, by the methods suggested, these seeds can not be destroyed without disadvantage before spring, the best plan to adopt will be to burn off as soon as possible after the grass is killed by frost; by this means some of the seeds are destroyed by fire, some by ice, and the balance being exposed, will feel the warmth much earlier, and will germinate in time to be destroyed by plowing, providing the plowing is delayed long enough. This method is almost as objectionable as mowing and burning in the fall, as the plowing is delayed till March, the planting is late, and all the benefit of the August market is lost; but it is still in my opinion the most advantageous plan. The grass seeds are in the ground, producing a hardier and more prolific plant than rice. The man who calculates that they will not come up, finds out his mistake too late to remedy it, except at considerable cost.

Hand weeding.—Hand weeding is out of the question, being too slow and expensive for the large planter. One of the great advantages of hand weeding consists in pulling the grass up by the roots, which, while it effectually destroys the grass, loosens up the land, and when properly done is equivalent to a thorough working. This requires considerable slight-of-hand and care, and is the kind of work that can not be done by inexperienced hired labor.

Rice comes nearer to being a cultivated crop in the lower part of Plaquemines Parish than in any other part of this State. It is claimed down there that rice never thrives until after it is weeded; and we can readily see the reason, for in tearing up the grass-roots, the soil is loosened and put into condition so that the rice roots can penetrate it and secure a bountiful supply of nutriment. But this kind of cultivation is too expensive for the large planter, and his only resource, if caught with a grassy crop, is to mow everything and trust to the rapid growth of the rice to smother out its slower growing rivals. This it generally does, but its race for life absorbs all of its energies and gives it no time to sucker, thus materially reducing the yield. When our lands were new 15 barrels per acre was about an average yield on a large place, while now we consider 10 barrels about the standard. This great falling off in a few years is not owing so much to the exhaustion of the soil as to the grass crop in our rice, which chokes out the stand and prevents what is left from suckering, and to the neglect of drainage in the fall and winter. As I stated before, the most successful means I have used for keeping my fields clean is to burn off early and let the grass come up before plowing. If a clean stand can be secured it will not be necessary to mow, as a few weeds can be cut out with a cane knife. The crop can be harvested fully two weeks earlier, and a better yield obtained. While fall plowing is advantageous in turning the land up and giving it a chance to drain, it is equally disadvantageous in covering up not only the grass seed, but the scattered rice and protecting it through the winter. I have tried this repeatedly with four-horse plows, and failed in every instance to derive any benefit.

The practice of following rice with winter oats after mowing and burning the stubble and aftermath has been favorably suggested.

SOUTHWESTERN LOUISIANA AND SOUTHEASTERN TEXAS.

It is necessary to treat of rice production in this section separately, because the methods are in some respects different from those practiced in any other portion of the world.

METHODS OF RICE CULTURE REVOLUTIONIZED.

The revolution in the methods of growing rice has been as great as that caused by the introduction of modern agricultural machinery into the wheat fields, which has given the United States control of the markets of the world.

In 1884 and 1885 a few farmers from the Northwestern prairie States settled on the great southern prairie which extends along the coast from the parish of St. Mary in Louisiana to the Texas line, about 140 miles. Finding that rice, which had been grown for many years for home consumption, but by oriental methods, was well suited to the conditions of agriculture here, they commenced immediately to adapt the agricultural machinery to which they had been accustomed to the rice industry. The gang plow, disc harrow, drill, and broadcast seeder were readily adjusted, but the twine binder encountered a number of serious obstacles. However, by the close of 1886 the principal difficulties had been overcome. Wherever prairies were found sufficiently level, with an intersecting creek which could be used to flood them, they were surrounded by a small levee thrown up by a road grader or by a plow with a strong wing attached to the mold board extending it 4 or 5 feet. Very few interior ditches were made for drainage. The land was so level that fields of 40 and 80 acres were common. Large crops were produced, the prairies were practically free from injurious grasses, and the creek or river water was soft and bore no damaging seeds to the fields. The rice fields were handled like the bonanza wheat farms of Dakota, and fortunes were made. Levees were cheaply constructed; little attention was paid to drainage more than to remove the surface water; shocking, stacking and threshing were done in a very careless manner; the main object being apparently to plant a large acreage and secure a certain number of bushels, regardless of quality. Ultimate failure was certain, but it was hastened by drought. A succession of dry years followed. The creeks failed, and reservoirs were found to be expensive and unreliable.

The soil and climatic conditions in southeastern Texas are almost precisely like those in southwestern Louisiana. Rice culture in this section requires no separate treatment. What is applicable to the one applies also to the other. There is a belt of prairie well suited to rice extending from the Sabine River west for 100 miles along the coast. Within a few years large farms have been opened and devoted to this cereal with excellent returns.

IRRIGATION.

Pumping plants.—To provide a reliable supply of water, plants for pumping (Plate I) were gradually substituted for the natural irrigation relied on to produce a crop on the so-called "providence rice farms." Fortunately the water in the rivers is soft, abundant, and free

PLATE I.

PUMPING PLANT FOR RICE-IRRIGATING CANAL.

from silt and damaging weed seeds. The elevation of the prairies above the streams varies from 6 to 38 feet, the larger portion being from 15 to 25 feet. At first farms along the streams and lakes were irrigated; gradually large surface canals were constructed.

Canals for irrigation.—Irrigating canals were started in a small way in Acadia Parish in 1890. In 1894 a canal 40 feet wide was built for 15 miles with 10 miles of laterals. This was followed by the Crowley Canal, which is now 35 feet wide and 8 miles in length, and has 10 miles of lateral lines. The Riverside Canal was the next, and now has several miles in operation. These enterprises have grown steadily until there are now 9 canals in Acadia Parish, with an approximate length of 115 miles. There are about 25 irrigating canals in Acadia, Calcasieu, Cameron, and Vermilion parishes, with a total length of over 400 miles of mains and probably twice that extent of laterals, built at a total cost of about $1,500,000. In nearly every township there are one or more ridges slightly above the surrounding land. On these surface canals are built from 20 to 150 feet in width, according to the area to be watered. The sides of the canal are raised from 4 to 5 feet with plows and scrapers or with grading machinery. Grading machines work very well, as the soil is a loam or a clay loam free from stones. Side gates are inserted in the embankment as frequently as necessary. Laterals are run from the main canal to accommodate remote farms. Powerful pumping plants are erected on the bank of the river at the head of the surface canal. These canals, where well constructed and operated, prove entirely successful and make the rice crop a practical certainty over a large section of country. They range in irrigating capacity from 1,000 to 30,000 acres. The usual water rent charged the planter by the canal company is 324 pounds of rough rice per acre watered.

Cost of canals.—The cost of constructing permanent canals is considerable. Between the river or lake bank, at the initial point, and the general level of the table lands, and in crossing occasional depressions the levees must be both high and wide at the base. The canal must run upon a divide in order that it may not cross any streams and may be sufficiently above the general level to water all portions of the adjacent country. The lands where the levee is to be constructed should be thoroughly plowed before excavation is commenced; otherwise the fresh dirt placed upon the sod does not sufficiently cement to prevent seepage.

Outlets.—The outlets for flooding the fields must be carefully protected or the crawfish will dig under the gates from the inside and cause a crevasse. A very successful plan is to bed a sill 4 by 6 inches in size across the bottom of the opening near the inner end and level with the bottom, allowing the ends of the sill to project into the bank on either side of the opening 6 feet; then plank along the inner side of the sill the full length, using boards 3 feet long, with the top of the boards resting against and even with the sill. The boards should stand at an angle of 45°, the lower ends being near the center of the canal. At each end of this planking a board of the same length and about 12 inches wide should be nailed at a right angle with the planking, thus projecting downward into the earth. Posts should be set against the sill at each side of the cut and at the ends, and the boarding from the sill to the top of the bank should be solid except at the outlet. A 12-inch board should be nailed at a right angle with the face of the cribbing back into the bank at the end of the sills to stop crawfish. The opening should be boarded on the sides and bottom, and this should extend 6 feet outside the cut to prevent undermining from the overflow. The gate may be raised by a lever or otherwise. Openings thus constructed are proof against damage by crawfish.

When a large number of planters are drawing their supply of water from the same canal some will use more than is necessary and increase the expense of the general supply. Some plant very early and require water a month before the general crop is ready. These and other incidents can generally be settled with little friction.

Deep wells for irrigation.—Scarcely had the surface canals been accepted as a success when southwestern Louisiana was startled by the announcement that there were strata of gravel at 125 to 200 feet under the surface of the entire section containing an unlimited supply of water which would, of its own pressure, come so near the surface that it could be readily pumped. This was received with considerable incredulity at first, but repeated tests have proved that there is a bed of gravel nearly 50 feet in thickness underlying this section of Louisiana which carries a large amount of soft water with sufficient pressure to bring it nearly to the surface. Pipes of 2, 3, 4, 6, and 8-inch size have been sunk to the gravel and pumped continuously for months without diminution of the supply. The water is soft, at a constant temperature of about 70 degrees, and absolutely free from injurious seeds or minerals. Such is the facility with which these wells are made that a 6-inch tube has been put down to the full depth required—200 feet—in fourteen hours. Thus far it has been found that a 2-inch pipe will furnish sufficient water to flood 10 acres of rice and a 6-inch pipe will flood 80 to 90 acres. Any number of wells may be made, and even if no more than 20 or 30 feet apart one does not diminish the amount of water obtained from the other. It is probable that such wells will become common for the irrigation of other crops than rice.

Hon. S. L. Cary says:

Wells from 2 to 12 inches can be put down successfully. From 50 to 100 such wells are in successful operation in the rice belt of southwestern Louisiana. Passing through alternate layers of clay and quicksand, coarse water-bearing gravel is reached at the depth of 100 to 150 feet. Forty feet of screened pipe reaching into this gravel is sufficient. A 6-inch well will furnish a constant stream for a 4 to 5 inch pump. A system of such wells may be put down 10 to 40 feet apart and each one will act independently and furnish as much water as if it stood alone. Such a combination of wells may be united just below wat r level and all be run by one engine and pump. Water rises naturally in these wells to within 20 feet of the surface, and a number of flowing wells have been secured. The lift is not greater than from rivers, lakes, or bayous into canals. Eight 4-inch wells united at the top can be run by one 16-inch pump and a 50-horsepower engine, and will flood 1,000 acres of rice. With present conditions there are good profits to the grower. Water is the largest factor in rice production, and we are prepared to take the advice of the millionaire, "Sell water."

The total cost of an irrigating plant sufficient for flooding 200 acres is from $1,500 to $2,500. It requires about seventy days' pumping for the rice season.

DRAINAGE.

Danger from alkali.—Thorough drainage is even more essential for rice than for wheat, because irrigation brings the alkali to the surface to an extent that finally becomes detrimental to the rice plant. Alkali sometimes accumulates in the soil just below the depth of the usual furrow to such an extent that any plowing is dangerous to the crop. Experience has shown that there is but one effective way of disposing of these salts, and that is by thorough drainage and deep plowing. As the water drains away the excess of soluble salts is carried off. Now, if the ditches are no deeper than the ordinary furrow it is evident that only the surface of the soil can be cleared. Until tiling can be employed the use of plenty of open ditches, at least 3 feet deep for mains, must be the chief reliance of the rice farmer in his fight against the accumulation of alkali in the surface soil.

Ditches.—The construction of levees for drainage ditches is a simple process as compared with the old system of using the spade and shovel. A plow with an extension moldboard, or winged scraper about 5 feet long, is generally used. Some use a plow followed by a V scraper made of plank, which removes the dirt from the furrow 4 or 5 feet to the right or to the left as the case may be, thus forming a ridge or levee. The broader ditch thus made is less liable to be choked with grasses than ditches made with a spade or capstan ditching plow. Usually not more than 1 foot of drainage is obtained with such implements. This is ample for removing surface water, but does not give sufficient depth for thorough drainage to put the field in the best condition for cultivation in the early spring.

HIGH-LAND VERSUS LOW-LAND RICE.

Where exclusively wet cultivation is employed, i. e., plowing and sowing in water on lowland, the rice is considerably inferior to that produced upon soil well drained and thoroughly tilled. Rice follows the law so well established for wheat, oats, and other cereals, that thorough cultivation not only increases the quantity produced per acre, but improves the quality and flavor of the grain. It has been claimed by some that rice, being a water plant, does not follow this rule. This is an error. The rice of commerce is an improved variety, far superior to wild rice, and the improvement has come through better environment. We have not yet reached the limit of possible improvement in rice by this means.

The following statement by H. R. Williams, jr., of Canton, China, shows the opinion of Chinese merchants as to the relative merits of upland and low-land rice:

Rice grown on high lands is better than that grown on low lands on about a level with the rivers, and brings a higher price. Furthermore, there is more nutriment in the high-land rice, as the Chinese say they get as much satisfaction from a catty of high-land rice as from 1¼ catties of that grown on low land. All of the high-land rice is irrigated from large ponds. Rice grown upon low land is of course supplied with water from the rivers as they rise and fall. The high-land rice is a smaller grain but is harder and heavier than the low-land rice.

In Japan the cultivation of rice is more thorough. the soils are better drained during the winter than in most countries, and the product is so superior in quality and flavor that imported rices can not be sold to the Japanese in competition with their home product.

Thorough winter drainage enables the planter to plow and sow sufficiently early to harvest before the equinoctial storms and to get the benefit of the early market.

GENERAL NOTES ON CULTURE AND TREATMENT OF RICE.

PREPARING THE GROUND.

Some planters advocate shallow plowing for rice because it appears to thrive best in compact earth. Even if it be granted that the rice plant finds a more favorable condition in compact earth, it does not prove the superiority of shallow over deep plowing. It has been demonstrated that the better the soil and the more thoroughly it is pulverized the better the crop. The roots of annual cultivated plants do not feed much below the plow line, so that it becomes evident that deep cultivation places more food within the reach of the plant. If pulverizing the earth deeply be a disadvantage, by reason of the too great porosity of the soil at seeding time, it can be easily remedied by the use of a heavy roller subsequently. If the soil is well drained, deep plowing will be found profitable. Deep plowing just before planting sometimes brings too much alkali to the surface. The remedy for this is to plow a little deeper than the previous plowing just after harvest; the alkali will then be washed out before the spring plowing. The plow should be followed in a short time by the disk harrow and then by the smoothing harrow. If the land is allowed to remain in the furrow for any considerable time it will bake and can not be brought into that fine tilth so necessary to the best seed conditions. This is particularly true of rice land. If the best results are desired, it will be advisable to follow the harrrow with a heavy roller. The roller will crush the lumps, make the soil more compact, and conserve the moisture for germinating the grain, rendering it unnecessary to flood for "sprouting."

SOWING.

Selecting the seed.—Too great care can not be exercised in selecting rice for seed. It is indispensable that the seed should be free from red rice, uniform in quality and size of kernel, well filled, flinty, free from sun cracks, and free from all foreign seeds. Uniformity of kernel is more essential in rice than in other cereals, because of the polishing process.

Drilling.—The rice should be planted with a drill. It will be more equally distributed and the quantity used to the acre will be exact. The seeds will be planted at a uniform depth and the earth packed over them by the roller. It also prevents the birds from taking the seeds. The roller should precede the drill. If it follows the drill the feet of the horses, mules, or oxen drawing the roller will press some of the planted rice 4 or 5 inches deeper into the earth than the general average. Furthermore, the lumps of earth will prevent the uniform operation of the drill. In rice farming too much emphasis can not be placed upon the importance of thoroughly pulverizing the soil to a considerable depth; leveling with a harrow as perfectly as possible; crushing all the lumps and packing the surface to conserve the moisture, and planting the seed at a uniform depth.

Broadcast sowing.—Broadcast sowing of rice should be discontinued; the seed is never scattered with uniformity; some grains remain upon the surface and the remainder is buried by the harrow and the tramp of the team to depths varying from 1 to 6 inches. Rice sown broadcast does not germinate with any uniformity. Some seeds are taken by the birds, some are too near the surface and lack moisture to germinate, while others are buried too deep. In some instances the variation in the germination of the rice in the same field has been as much as eight weeks. Then at the harvest when the main portion is ready for the reaper, quite an amount of the rice is still immature. The product commands a very low price in the market, because the merchantable grain must sell at the price of the low grade. Care must be taken to plant the several fields at different periods, so that the harvest will not be too crowded. It requires much more care to produce a strictly first-class quality of rice than is found necessary in the production of any other cereal, and nearly every fall prime offerings are the exception.

INJURY TO BLOOM.

If it is very showery during the period of bloom, pollination is frequently incomplete with consequent reduction in the crop. This rarely occurs with early planted rice. Occasionally the rice crop suffers from severe storms about the period of ripening. Fortunately these disasters are mainly local and limited to the equinoctial period. Otherwise rice has few enemies and may be regarded as the most reliable of all cereal crops. On this account, as well as for its food value, it has been adopted as the staple cereal in countries having a dense population, where any considerable failure of the crop would involve starvation for thousands.

FLOODING.

Depth of water.—Except where water is necessary for germinating the seed, flooding is not practiced until the rice is 6 to 8 inches high. If showers are abundant enough to keep the soil moist it is better to delay flooding till the rice is 8 inches high, as there is considerable danger of scalding the rice when very young. At 8 inches high a sufficient depth of water can be allowed on the field to prevent scalding. The depth of water that should be maintained from the first flooding until it is withdrawn for the harvest depends upon other conditions. If the growing crop thoroughly shades the land, just water enough to keep the soil saturated will answer. To be safe, however, for all portions of the field, it should stand 3 to 6 inches deep, and, to avoid stagnation, it should be renewed by a continuous inflow and outflow. In case the stand of rice is thin the water should be deeper. A flow of water through the field aids in keeping the body of the water cool and in preventing the growth of injurious plants that thrive in the stagnant water. The water should stand at uniform depth all over the field. Unequal depths of water will cause the crop to ripen at different times.

Uniform ripening.—The planter should particularly note the importance of not making the fields too large. It impedes complete drainage. It is inconvenient to have large ditches intersecting the fields. The simultaneous maturity of all portions of the field is desirable if it is to be cut with a twine binder. This can be secured by uniform and good drainage, by plowing, harrowing, planting, and rolling the same day, and by planting the seed equally deep and evenly distributed. The flooding water must stand in all portions of the field at equal depth and temperature. Emphasis is placed upon having the harrow closely follow the plow, to be immediately succeeded by planting and rolling. This is necessary to conserve the moisture, unless there are frequent showers during the planting season. No field should be so large that the work of planting can not be completed within three or four days.

Time to withdraw the water and to cut the grain.—As soon as the grain is in the dough the water should be withdrawn. Sufficient moisture will remain in the soil to mature the crop. Experiments with wheat have demonstrated that there is a considerable gain in commercial value by cutting nearly two weeks before the grain is dead ripe; i. e., when the straw is yellow and the kernel still in the stiff dough state. The Japanese apply the same principle in cutting rice; it is cut when the straw has barely commenced to yellow. If cutting is delayed till the straw shows yellow to the top the grain is reduced in quality and quantity and the straw is less valuable. There is also a considerable increase in the loss by shelling in handling in the field.

PLATE II.

HARVESTING RICE IN SOUTHWESTERN LOUISIANA.

PLATE III.

THRASHING RICE IN SOUTHWESTERN LOUISIANA.

HARVESTING.

When rice is ready for the harvest (Plate II), cutting should proceed rapidly. If a field requires more than four days to complete the cutting it is too large, and should be divided. The length of straw to be cut is a matter of option with each planter, but if cut in the stiff-dough state of the kernel sufficient straw must remain with the head to enable the grains to mature. On an average 2½ feet of straw will be found practical. The smaller the bundle the better for curing. In case the field is wet the bundles should be taken from the reaper direct to high land and there shocked. While care should be exercised in all the various processes of rice production, it is most necessary in shocking, which is generally left to some boy who can do nothing else. Thirty per cent of the crop may be lost by improper shocking. The following directions will aid: First, shock on dry ground; second, brace the bundles carefully against each other, so as to resist wind or storm; third, let the shock be longest east and west and cap carefully with bundles, allowing the heads of the capping bundles to fall on the north side of the shock to avoid the sun. Exposure of the heads to sun and storm is a large factor in producing sun-cracked and chalky kernels, which reduce the milling value. The idea is slow curing in the shade to produce that toughness of kernel necessary to withstand the milling processes. In the shock every head should be shaded and sheltered from storm as much as possible. The rice should be left in the shock till the straw is cured and the kernel hard.

Whether stacking rice from the shock is a benefit depends upon the condition of the grain and straw at the time of stacking and how the stacking is done. If too much heat is generated, stacking is an injury. It is, moreover, of less importance with rice than with wheat. Judging from the practice in other countries, rice well cured in the shock and aired after thrashing ought to keep in the bin without heating.

THRASHING.

With the large steam thrashers (Plate III) there is frequently considerable breakage and waste of grain. Great care should be exercised to avoid this and preserve every part which has been won from the soil with such labor. At the commencement of thrashing, examination should be made to see that there is no avoidable breakage of the grain. If the rice is damp when delivered from the machine it should be spread upon a floor and dried before sacking, so as to be in the best condition for the market, for color of grain affects the value.

FERTILIZING.

It has been claimed that the flooding of the rice fields restores to the soil as much nutritive material as the rice crop removes. Where lands are flooded from rivers like the Mississippi or the Nile, which carry a large amount of silt, this may be true. It is not the case where flooding is done with pure water. The continued fertility of the rice field can only be maintained by restoring to the soil annually a portion of what the crop removes. Whether this can be more economically done by the use of commercial fertilizers and plowing under of the rice straw or by fallowing occasionally and using some renovating crop as a green manure is an economic question to be determined by each planter according to the conditions presented. Repeated trials of commercial fertilizers have almost invariably shown gains in the quality and quantity of the crop more than sufficient to cover the cost. Summer fallowing, where it can be practiced, is, in addition to its renovating effect, a substantial aid in destroying noxious grasses and red rice. It appears to be a general impression that red rice can be destroyed by allowing the field to remain without crop for a few years and pasturing with sheep or hogs. In one well-established case this was tried for eight years, and at the expiration of that period the field was plowed and still produced red rice. Close grazing is helpful, but where summer fallowing can be employed it is far more advantageous than grazing.

EXPERIMENTS IN JAPAN.

There is very little exact information on the subject of fertilizers for rice. In Japan and other oriental countries a large proportion of the rice lands is thoroughly fertilized in the fall with straw, leaves, rice hulls, fish, and night soil. The fields are planted to wheat or vetches for the winter crop, followed the next spring by rice without additional manures. While carefully done, there are no comparisons or data to show the actual advantage of fall fertilization to the rice crop. At the Imperial College of Agriculture at Tokio, Japan, a series of experiments has been conducted on the same plats for nine years to determine the elements best suited to increase the yield of rice in Japanese soils. Four small plats were selected, planted with the same variety of rice, and treated in every way alike except in the application of fertilizers. For nine consecutive years a small amount of phosphate and potash was sown on plat No. 1; on plat 2, equal amounts of phosphoric acid and nitrogen; on plat 3, potash and nitrogen; on plat 4, potash, nitrogen, and phosphate. All these fertilizers were in an easily convertible form. At the expiration of the test the rice on plats 1 and 2 was medium in quality and quantity. That on plat 3 was very poor—could scarcely be called a crop—and that on plat 4 was very much superior to all of the others, clearly indicating the value of a complete fertilizer containing the three essential elements of plant food—nitrogen, potash, and phosphoric acid.

In Bulletins 15 and 24 of the Louisiana Experiment Station Dr. W. C. Stubbs has discussed this subject of manures for rice. He says:[1]

Rice is not a great impoverisher of the soil, especially if the straw and chaff are regularly returned to it. Exactly how to apply manures to rice in order that they may accomplish the greatest amount of good possible, when the rice is soon to be inundated, is yet an unsettled question. For the two years of the experiment the various fertilizers have been scattered broadcast over the soil before being broken. The soil has then been inverted and harrowed and rice sown. This mode of application has not been satisfactory. The increased results, while sometimes apparent, were not large.

The largest yield was obtained from an application of 300 pounds of cotton-seed meal, 150 pounds of acid phosphate, and 50 pounds of kainit spread on the surface of the plowed ground just before the seed was harrowed in. The same fertilizers used singly or in combinations of only two did not increase the yield of either straw or grain when spread on the ground and plowed under. The increase for the first mixture amounted to 25 per cent of both straw and grain. Where plowed under, the fertilizers seem to have been buried too deep to produce any noticeable effect.

While these conclusions are not final, Dr. Stubbs recommends the use on black soils of two parts of cotton-seed meal and one part acid phosphate, mixed and applied broadcast before the rice is harrowed in. On sandy land he would add kainit at the rate of 200 pounds to the acre. In Bulletin 24 there is the following additional report:[2]

On April 25, 1898, the ground was broken and harrowed, fertilizer distributed broadcast, rice sown, and both harrowed in together. This was nicely accomplished by harrowing both ways. The following are the experiments with manures used per acre:

Plat No. 1. No fertilizer, yielded 1,382 pounds of grain.
Plat No. 2. Seventy-five pounds sulphate of ammonia, yielded 1,392 pounds of grain.
Plat No. 3. Three hundred pounds cotton-seed meal and 150 pounds acid phosphate, yielded 1,664 pounds of grain.
Plat No. 4. Seventy-five pounds dried blood and 37 pounds bone meal, yielded 1,543 pounds of grain.
Plat No. 5. No fertilizer, yielded 1,056 pounds of grain.
Plat No. 6. Two hundred pounds cotton-seed meal, yielded 1,344 pounds of grain.
Plat No. 7. Two hundred pounds cotton-seed meal and 100 pounds acid phosphate, yielded 1,881 pounds of grain.
Plat No. 8. One hundred pounds of cotton-seed meal, 25 pounds of fish scrap, 25 pounds nitrate of soda, and 100 pounds of acid phosphate, yielded 1,677 pounds of grain.
Plat No. 9. No fertilizer, yielded 1,559 pounds of grain.

These results are quite unsatisfactory, because there is a wide divergence in the yield between the best and poorest unfertilized plots. The difference in yield between plots 9 and 7 is not so marked as between 9 and 5, and the increase from the use of ·the best of the fertilizers amounts to little more than the cost of the application.

[1] Bul. 15, p. 4. 1888.   [2] Bul. 24, p. 365. 1889.

It is quite probable that the yield depends as much on the thorough aeration of the soil and the abundance of the organic matter present as on the mineral elements. Complete drainage in winter, followed by deep plowing and then disking, harrowing, and rolling until the seed bed is fine, will probably serve better to increase the yield than an application of the best commercial fertilizers without proper cultivation. This can be supplemented by an occasional summer crop of cowpeas or velvet beans to supply humus and organic nitrogen.

SOILS ADAPTED TO RICE.

The best soil for rice is a medium loam, containing about 50 per cent of clay. This allows the presence of sufficient humus for the highest fertility without decreasing too much the compact nature of the soil. The alluvial lands along the Southern rivers, where they can be drained, are well adapted to rice cultivation. Occasionally such lands are too sandy. The rich drift soils of the Louisiana and Texas prairies have shown a marvelous adaptation to rice. These soils are underlaid with clay so as to be retentive of water. The sand is exceedingly fine. There is about the right proportion of potash, phosphoric acid, other essential mineral elements, and humus to be lastingly productive. They are sufficiently remote from the coast to be free from devastating storms and the serious attack of birds. There is no expensive clearing, ditching, or leveeing to prepare the lands for rice. The drainage is good and the lands can be cultivated to winter crops, thus preventing the growth of red rice and injurious weeds and grasses. Such cultivation enables the planter to plow deeply in the fall and fertilize. Plowing when done in the spring should be shallow. Rice roots are not deep feeders. Showing its wide range of adaptation, rice from the same sack has been planted in moist land and flooded; in cultivated upland fields and on levees 18 inches above the water. For a time it grew with almost equal vigor under each of the foregoing conditions. The principal difference appeared in the maturing of the seed. Trials have been made with soils covered with a large amount of decayed vegetation. The results were generally disappointing. The roots of the rice, being shallow feeders, did not gain much hold upon the soil, and the proportion of mineral matter and silicates in the decayed vegetation was not adapted to the rice plant. Rice has generally failed on peaty soils.

Gravelly or sandy soils are not adapted to rice cultivation because they do not possess the mechanical conditions for the retention of water. Occasionally, on a light sandy soil, underlaid by a stiff subsoil, one or two fairly good crops of rice may be secured, but this is the limit.

WAGES AND EFFICIENCY OF LABOR IN DIFFERENT COUNTRIES.

The great variations in wages and in the area which can be cultivated by the laborer in different countries are shown in the following table:

Number of acres one man can farm in rice, with wages, in different countries.

Countries.	Acres.	Farm wages in gold per year, with board.	Countries.	Acres.	Farm wages in gold per year, with board.
Japan	½	$10 to $18	Spain	5	$40 to $60
China	½ to 2½	8 to 12	United States:		
Philippines	2½	15 to 20	Carolinas	8	96 to 120
India	3	10 to 20	Mississippi delta	10	120 to 144
Siam	3	10 to 20	Southwestern Louisiana and Texas	80	180 to 216
Egypt	4	15 to 30			
Italy	5	40 to 60			

PRIMITIVE RICE MILLING.

The primitive method of milling rice was to place a small quantity in a hollow stone or block of wood and pound it with a pestle. The blow with the pestle cracked the hull, and the friction created by the sliding motion of the rice under the blow removed the hull and the cuticle. The bran and hulls were then removed by winnowing. The first advance upon this primitive mechanical process was to make the receptacle for the rice out of a short section of a hollow log, using a heavy wooden pounder bound to a horizontal beam 6 to 8 feet long, resting on a fulcrum 4 to 5 feet from the pounder. The pounder was raised by stepping on the short end of the beam, and by suddenly removing the weight the pounder dropped into the rice tub and delivered a blow. The end of the pounder was concave with edges rounded. This simple machine and the fanning mill are in common use in oriental countries to this day.

As one passes along the street in an oriental city, a peculiar sound is brought to the ear as of a blow delivered upon some yielding substance. Looking to the right or left one sees a rice mill, consisting of a one-man power jumping on and off the beam of the pounder and one-woman power at a crude fanning mill cleaning the grain. Such a mill cleans about 11 bushels (a trifle over 3 barrels) of paddy rice per day, at a cost of 6 cents (gold) per barrel.

In time water power was used to turn an overshot wheel, which was geared to a long horizontal shaft with arms at distances apart equal to that of the rice pounders. The rice pounder was a vertical beam about 10 feet long and 6 inches square, with a pin projecting at a point to be caught by the rounded end of the arm of the revolving shaft, which raised the pounder a short distance then slipped past the pin, allowing the pounder to drop into the tub of rice. This process was repeated until the hull and bran were removed. The rice tubs stood in a row as closely as practicable for use. Generally, to economize space, there were two shafts revolving in opposite directions, allowing two rows of rice tubs. In every mountain village in Japan such mills may be found preparing the rice for local consumption. They usually have about eight pounders and mill 96 bushels daily, or 26⅔ barrels, of paddy rice, at a cost of about 2 cents per barrel, which is more than paid for by the offal. In cities steam power is used and the number of pounders greatly increased, but the process is practically unchanged.

COMMERCIAL RICE MILLING.

The usual process.—The processes of milling rice are quite complicated. The paddy is first screened to remove trash and foreign particles. The hulls, or chaff, are removed by rapidly revolving "milling stones" set about two-thirds of the length of a rice grain apart. The product goes over horizontal screens and blowers, which separate the light chaff and the whole and broken kernels. The grain is now of a mixed yellow and white color. To remove the outer skin the grain is put in huge mortars holding from 4 to 6 bushels each and pounded with pestles weighing 350 to 400 pounds. Strange to say, the heavy weight of the pestle breaks very little grain.

When sufficiently decorticated, the contents of the mortars, consisting now of flour, fine chaff, and clean rice of a dull, filmy, creamy color, are removed to the flour screens, where the flour is sifted out. From thence the rice and fine chaff go to the fine-chaff fan, where the fine chaff is blown out and mixed with the other flour. The rice flour, as we call it, or more properly "rice meal," as our English neighbors call it, is very valuable as stock feed, being rich in carbohydrates as well as albuminoids.

From the fine-chaff fan the rice goes to the cooling bins, rendered necessary by the heavy frictional process through which it has just passed. It is allowed to remain here for eight or nine hours, and then passes to the brush screens, whence the smallest rice and what little flour is left pass down one side and the larger rice down the other.

The grain is now clean and ready for the last process—polishing. This is necessary to give the rice its pearly luster, and it makes all the difference imaginable in its appearance. The polishing is effected by friction against the rice of pieces of moose hide or sheepskin tanned and worked to a wonderful degree of softness, loosely tacked around a double cylinder of wood and wire gauze. From the polishers the rice goes to the separating screens, composed of different sizes of gauze, where it is divided into its appropriate grades. It is then barreled and is ready for market.

An improved process.—In mills more recently erected the foregoing process has been modified by substituting the "huller" for the mortar and pounder. The huller is a short, cast iron, horizontal tube with interior ribs and a funnel at one end to admit the rice. Within this tube revolves a shaft with ribs. These ribs are so adjusted that the revolution of the shaft creates the friction necessary to remove the cuticle. The rice passes out of the huller at the end opposite the funnel. It resembles externally a large sausage machine. It requires six hullers for each set of burs. The automatic sacker and weigher is used instead of barreling, sacks being preferred for shipping the cleaned rice. Sheepskins are used for polishing.

With the above modification of the milling processes considerable reduction has been made in the cost of the mill. Mills of a daily capacity of 60,000 pounds of cleaned rice can now be constructed at a total cost of $10,000 to $15,000.

A portable mill.—A portable rice mill has also been devised for plantation use, costing $250, aside from the power to run it, and capable of cleaning 8,100 pounds of paddy rice per day. Such small machines do not give the finish required by the general market, but turn out excellent rice for local use.

EFFECTS OF FASHION IN RICE.

It is to be regretted that fashion has so much to do with rice. It requires a high gloss, and to obtain this the most nutritious portions are removed under the polishing process. Estimated according to the food values, rice polish is 1.76 times as valuable for food as polished rice. The oriental custom, much used by farmers in the South, of removing the hulls and bran with a pounder and using the grain without polishing is economical and furnishes a rice of much higher food value than the rice of commerce. In the process of polishing nearly all the fats are removed. In 100 pounds of rice polish there are 7.2 pounds of fats. In 100 pounds of polished rice there is only 0.38 pound of fat. Upon the theory that the flavor is in the fats it is easy to understand the lack of it in commercial rice, and why travelers universally speak of the excellent quality of the rice they eat in oriental countries.

Grades and prices.—Aside from the loss in flavor and nutritive value by polishing, fashion again increases the cost of commercial rice by demanding whole grains and places a value of about 2 cents per pound more on head rice (whole grains) than on the same quality slightly broken. The weekly New Orleans market report for June 3, 1899, makes the following quotations on cleaned rice per pound:

	Cents.		Cents.
Fancy	6	Ordinary	3
Choice	5¼	Common	2¼
Good	4¼	Inferior	1¾
Fair	3¾	No. 2	1½

These grades are determined not by the difference in quality, but by appearance, and may be manufactured from the same quality of paddy rice. Ordinarily a choice lot of paddy would yield three qualities of rice: Whole grains grading "fancy," "choice," or "good;" "fair" or "ordinary;" and No. 2, consisting of fragments and broken grains.

The president of the New Orleans Board of Trade, Hon. S. Lock Breaux, states that "the basis of grades of clean rice is predicated upon the size of the bean, its brilliancy (high polish), and general appearance, each lot presenting individual characteristics that to the buyer add or detract from its normal value." The following official quotations of the New Orleans Board of Trade for June 16, 1899, are in point:

Spot quotations, per pound, clean; quiet but steady:

No. 2	1⅝ to 1¾
Inferior	1¾ to 2
Common	2½ to 3
Screenings	2 to 2¾
Ordinary	3 to 3¾
Fair head	3¾ to 4¼
Good head	4¼ to 4¾
Prime head	4¾ to 5⅛
Choice head	5¼ to 5¾
Fancy head	6 to 6½
Extra fancy	6½ to 6¾

There may be a slight difference in food value between No. 2 (fine rice sold to brewers) and extra fancy, but if any it is trifling. If rice is to enter largely into the list of economic foods for the use of the masses, grades must be established based on the food values and not on the shine of the surface. It would be just as sensible to place a price on shoes according to the polish they will take.

LOSS BY BREAKAGE IN MILLING.

We are now prepared to understand the loss by breakage of the kernel in milling. If the grain remains whole and is sufficiently hard to receive a high polish it sells for 6½ cents per pound. If it breaks it drops in price 2 or 3 cents per pound, and if it crumbles so that the particles will pass through a No. 12 seive the price is 1⅝ cents per pound. The question is, What is the average breakage per 100 pounds and how can it be remedied? Investigations made among the rice millers in 1897 led to the conclusion (based upon their written statements) that the perfect grains were only about 40 per cent of the total product. Recent letters addressed to the various rice mills have failed in most cases to elicit the information. The president of the New Orleans Board of Trade states in a letter: "The second part of your letter we are unable to answer as a proposition, for the reason that different mills achieve different results, and there is no way by which the trade can arrive at an average of the yield made by the different mills, this information as a rule being carefully guarded." In the few reports received the grading of the milled product was so different that no conclusion could be drawn as to the relative amount obtained by the mills. In the mills reporting, the best lots of rice milled last season showed a breakage of 21½ to 40 per cent and the poorest lots showed from 65 to 100 per cent breakage. The best lots of rice gave from 100 to 112.9 pounds of milled rice from 162 pounds of paddy; the poorest gave only from 63.6 to 85 pounds from the same quantity of paddy.

RESULTS OF MILLING.

The following tables show the percentages obtained per barrel of 162 pounds by three different mills:

Report of a mill having a daily capacity of 1,200 barrels.

Grades.	In best lot.	In poorest lot.
	Pounds.	*Pounds.*
No. 1 or head rice	91.32	....
No. 2 or broken rice	15.30	59.82
Brewers' rice	6.28	3.78
Polish	8	16
Bran	20	40
Hulls	21.10	42.40
Total	162	162

This mill reports that during the milling season of 1898 Honduras rice averaged 85 pounds and Japan rice 95 pounds, total product from 162 pounds of paddy. The rice was below the average for other years.

Report of one of the largest mills in the United States.

Grades.	Best grade.	Medium grade.	Low grade.
	Pounds.	*Pounds.*	*Pounds.*
Head	70	55	30
Partly broken	15	20	25
Very broken	12	12	20
Brewers'	4	6	10
Total	101	93	85

Report of mill having a daily capacity of 200 barrels.

Grades.	In best lot.	In poorest lot.
	Pounds.	*Pounds.*
Head rice	60	....
Slightly broken	30	60
Very broken	10	15
Bran	25	35
Polish	5	8
Hulls	32	44
Total	162	162

NOTE.—There is a difference in these reports; one mill shows the best and poorest grades, and the others the best and poorest special lots milled. Two of the mills show that in the poorest lots of rice milled there was no head rice and the third mill reports only 30 pounds in low-grade rice.

Mr. G. G. Bauer, manager of the Lake Charles Rice Milling Co., states that:

Aside from the larger percentage of head produced by the better class of rough rices, its value in the clean, on account of its superior quality, is much greater than that of head produced from medium or low grades. It is for this additional reason that fine rough rices always command such comparatively big prices.

The total loss by breakage in the United States approximates $2,000,000 annually. A large proportion of this can be saved by selecting better seed; by more careful attention to field management in the production of the crop, and by more care in curing and threshing.

RICE MILLING IN EUROPE.

The United States consul at Bremen, Hon. George Keenan, writes as follows in regard to rice milling in Germany:

Form and value of the rice imported.—Rice is never imported into Bremen in the form of paddy in the strict sense of that term. It is mainly imported in the husk form, broken and whole, uncleaned. It has the shell on or part of it. It is in a similar condition to barley or oats taken from the thrasher, but often with less shell, depending upon the kind of rice. The Japan and Bengal rice has less shell when imported than the Siam or Burmah, and this is one reason why the former commands higher prices than the latter. The cost price in Japan is stated at $2.40 per 100 pounds; in Bengal, at $2.16 to $2.40 per 100 pounds; in Siam, at $1.20 to $1.40 per 100 pounds; in Burma, at $1.08 to $1.44 per 100 pounds. The cost price of course varies with the market and may be governed by the purchaser, the quantities and grades purchased, and the kind of connection the purchaser may have with the place of production.

Rice is always imported in sacks of about 100 pounds each. Freight rates from China to Bremen are $4.80 per ton by steamer; by sail, $1.92 to $2.16 per ton. The rates are governed largely by opportunity and competition in shipping. The largest concern in Bremen usually imports in its own vessels.

Cost of milling.—No reliable figures can be ascertained as to the cost of milling in Bremen. There are so many different grades of the paddy going to mill, and so many different grades of the milled rice produced, each at a different cost from the others, that detailed information regarding the whole would be necessary for an accurate conclusion. This it is impossible to get; at least the millers, if they know, are not disposed to impart the knowledge.

By-products.—The coarser part of the shell of the rice is used mainly for packing purposes. The finer part of the shell is cut up and mixed with the bran, and is used for cattle feed, as are the middlings or shorts. All of these by-products are consumed in Germany and sell, according to grade and quality, at from 22 cents to $1.40 per 100 pounds.

Work of the largest mills.—The largest mill in Bremen, which is said to be the largest of its kind in the world, uses engines of 800 to 900 horsepower, and 30 runs of stone; all of the shelling and grinding is done with the stone; the breaking or cracking of the rice ("skinning") is effected by steel rollers. The daily output of this mill, running twenty-four hours, is from 5,000 to 6,000 bags, each bag weighing 110 pounds. The yearly capacity is 125,000 tons, 500 hands are employed, and there is a capital stock of $3,200,000. The wage rate is from 75 cents to $1 a day. From 250,000 to 500,000 sacks of the unmilled product are in store constantly.

There are three others—one with a yearly capacity of 70,000 tons, with $700,000 capital, and working 300 hands; one with a yearly capacity of 40,000 tons, with $400,000 capital, and working 70 hands; the third about half the size of the last-named concern. Starch is the chief product of this mill, and the by-products are fed to cattle owned by the concern.

The total import into Bremen for the year 1896 was 412,834,237 pounds, valued at $5,534,282. The total export for the same period was 401,578,694 pounds, valued at $6,723,133. Freight rates from Bremen to New York on rice are—by steamer, $3.60 to $3.80 per ton; by sail, $1.08 to $1.20 per ton.

No intelligent information could be had concerning the number of pounds of whole rice, or broken, or fine broken rice passed through a No. 12 wire sieve. This point does not appear to have been estimated or measured by the millers here, at least they did not or could not give information concerning it.

As to the number of pounds of rice polish and rice bran obtained from 100 pounds of paddy and uncleaned, the estimate varies from 8 to 30 per cent, depending on the kind, quality, and condition of the rice, and also upon the degree of polish given it.

THE USES OF RICE.

RICE AS A FOOD.

As a food material rice is nutritious and easily digestible. In comparison with other grains it is poor in protein (albuminoids) and fat, and correspondingly rich in nonnitrogenous substances (carbohydrates).

RESULTS OF ANALYSES.

Analyses show that 100 pounds of rice contains 87.6 pounds of total nutriment, consisting of 7.4 pounds protein, 0.4 pound fat, and 79.4 pounds carbohydrates. In comparison with this 100 pounds of wheat flour contains 87.5 pounds of total nutriment, consisting of 11 pounds protein, 1.1 pounds fat, and 74.9 pounds carbohydrates.[1]

The relative food values of rice and wheat, based solely on the amount of albuminoids they contain, are in the proportion of 10 to 19; based on the value of total nutritive material, the proportion is 87 to 82.54. The ease with which the deficiency of albuminoids and fats can be supplied from legumes and the almost absolute certainty of producing a crop every year are the principal reasons why rice is the staple food in many densely populated countries.

It is claimed that boiled rice is digestible in one hour, and hence is an admirable food for the last meal of the day. Rice should be at least three months old before it is used for food.

A SUBSTITUTE FOR POTATOES.

In rice-producing countries rice is used in the daily foods as a substitute for Irish potatoes and wheat bread. At every meal in oriental lands rice is the principal food. It is eaten alone with a little dried fish for seasoning. In well-to-do families bits of preserved ginger, beans boiled and preserved, with sauce, mushrooms, barley cake, and sweets are used as relishes with the rice. There is also generally a vegetable or fish soup with which boiled rice is eaten. In the rice districts of the United States rice is used in place of the Irish potato. Dyspeptics will find great relief in substituting boiled rice for potatoes. Rice polish, or flour, which is now sold at the mills at one-half to three-fourths of a cent per pound for cattle food, will, when appreciated, be in demand for human food. It contains 10.95 per cent of protein, in comparison with 7.4 per cent for the clean rice.

BY-PRODUCTS OF RICE CULTURE.

STRAW.

Rice straw is worth preserving. As a fodder for stock its value is about equal to good southern prairie hay. Rice straw contains 4.72 per cent crude protein, 32.21 per cent carbohydrates, and 1.87 per cent fats. The sweetness and excellent flavor of well-preserved rice straw adds very materially to its practical feeding value, because stock will

---

[1] Fourth Ann. Rept. Conn. Storrs Agric. Exp. Station, 1891.

consume large quantities of it. Digestion experiments have not been made with the straw or any of the by-products of rice milling. Rice bran contains 12.1 per cent protein, 8.8 per cent fat, and 59.4 per cent fiber and carbohydrates; rice hulls, 3.6 per cent protein, 0.7 per cent fat, 35.7 per cent fiber, and 38.6 per cent other carbohydrates; and rice polish, 11.7 per cent protein, 7.3 per cent fat, and 64.3 per cent fiber and carbohydrates.[1]

According to an estimate made by Dr. Stubbs, director of the Louisiana experiment station,[2] rice polish is worth $21.55 per ton; rice bran, $20.80; rice straw, $9.13; and rice hulls, $8.34. These values are taken assuming the same digestibility for the nutritive elements as for those contained in the by-products of wheat and other cereals.

HULLS.

It has been widely assumed that rice hulls have no practical feeding value. The usual practice of rice mills has been to burn them. It has even been asserted that they were pure silicates. The analysis does not confirm this claim. One hundred pounds of air-dried hulls yield ash 13.85 per cent, fats 0.85 per cent, fiber 38.15 per cent, protein 2.80 per cent, and carbohydrates 34.99 per cent.

They are so deficient in flavor that it is difficult to induce animals to eat them. If ground and mixed with some highly nitrogenous food they could be used, but the small percentage of digestible material in them renders them almost valueless for food. It is evidently more economical to use them as a fertilizer. For this purpose rice hulls are more valuable than wheat or oat straw. While they have less nitrogen, for most soils the ash compensates. In all rice-producing countries it is important to increase the porosity of the soils and to add to the humus they contain, for general crops. Rice hulls should be plowed under for this purpose.

Hulls make an excellent mulch for garden and orchard, and in stiff and unfrosted soils are of great value when plowed under in moderate quantities. The slow decomposition of hulls is here an advantage.

In Oriental countries the hulls or husks are removed at home by passing the paddy rice through small burs made of clay, or cement, and wood, and are then used by the farmer as a fertilizer. The cost of removing the hulls is balanced by their value as a manure and the reduced cost for sacks and freight to market. The hulls form about 20 per cent of the weight of paddy rice. If the average cost of sacks and freight to market be estimated at one-fourth of a cent per pound, the saving by removing the hulls on the farm would be $2\frac{1}{4}$ cents per bushel or 8.1 cents per barrel (162 pounds).

---

[1] Yearbook U. S. Dept. Agriculture, 1896, p. 607.
[2] Louisiana Agr. Exp. Sta. Bul. 24.

HULL ASHES.

In passing through rice-milling districts large quantities of hull ashes will be noticed. These have been very little used by farmers and gardeners under the general impression that they were of no value. One hundred pounds of hull ashes contain 0.82 pound of phosphoric acid and 0.93 pound of potash. There are many other better sources of potash and phosphoric acid. The amount contained in the hull ashes would not pay the cost of scattering them over the fields.

Calling the mineral matter in the whole plant 100 per cent, we have, as shown by analysis:

Percentage of ash in whole plant.

Parts of plant.	Ash, per cent.
In the stubble and root	36.08
In the straw and leaves	36.08
In the hull	14.20
In the cotyledon and epidermis	11.07
In the clean rice	1.94
Total	100

Calling the mineral matter in the paddy 100 per cent we have:

Percentage of ash in paddy rice.

Parts of fruit.	Ash, per cent.
In the husk	51.01
In the cotyledon and epidermis	42.03
In the clean rice	6.96
Total	100

The planter who burns his straw and sells his rice in the paddy loses 63.92 per cent of the total mineral matter of the crop. If the rice straw and the hulls be returned to the soil as manure, 86.36 per cent of the mineral matter of the crop will be restored, and the loss would be only 13.64 per cent. The present method of burning rice hulls can not be too severely condemned, but doubtless will be continued as long as rice is sold in the paddy. Rice milling machinery is too expensive and too complicated to be successfully and profitably operated upon the farms, but hulling is a process requiring very simple and inexpensive machinery. It can be done profitably upon the farm, and is done in most of the great rice-producing countries. There is a further advantage in removing the hull before shipment to market. Both the miller and the farmer can with greater exactness determine the quality of the grain. All uncertainty as to quality operates against the seller. Any broken rice resulting from the hulling would be retained and fed upon the farm. Chalky or sun-cracked grains, instead of decreasing the price of the entire crop, would generally break under the hulling process and be separated from the solid kernels, which would then sell for more than sufficient to compensate for any decrease in quantity. Such a system of marketing would require the planters to have good storage and do the hulling gradually through the year, as the product was required for milling. If the entire crop hulled should be placed upon the market at one time, as now, there would be great danger of destruction by the rice weevil while stored. The hard husk of paddy rice presents formidable difficulties to the attack of the weevil.

RED RICE.

Frequent allusion has been made to red rice. The presence of any red grains in milled rice lowers the grade and reduces the price. The history of field cultivation has been that if red rice once obtains a foothold in a field, it increases rapidly from year to year until its presence in the paddy causes a reduction in the price of the rice. Finally it may prevail to such an extent that the rice becomes unsalable. The land must then be cultivated in some other crop for two or three years until the red rice is entirely eradicated. The loss to the rice planters from red rice in the crop has been great.

BOTANICAL NAMES AND CHARACTERS.

Dr. George Watt, in his treatise on rice in India,[1] recognizes four botanical varieties of the wild rice of that country. One of these, *Oryza sativa* var. *rufipogon*, is the "red rice," so well known to southern planters.

Red rice is so called from the red color of the grains. In most cases the grain is colored a dark red through the entire substance. In other instances seeds may present any shade of color between the red and white; again, only the seed coat contains the coloring matter, and in this case the grain comes from the mill clean and white, or with little stripes of red where the coat has been imperfectly removed.

The leaves of the variety *rufipogon* are larger than those of the cultivated form. The inflorescence is longer, more slender, copiously branched, forming an *erect* head, in general appearance like some forms of Johnson grass. The heads bear fewer and smaller grains. The receptacle at the end of the pedicel, just below the grain, is thick and short, with ear-like rims. The white rice, or cultivated form, *Oryza sativa bengalensis*, produces a plumper, more rounded grain and spikelet, borne on a longer pedicel, the receptacle of which is only slightly distorted. The panicles are less erect. The red rice in its native habitat in India grows in drier places and requires much less water than the parent stock of the common white rice.

---

[1] Dictionary of the Econ. Prod. Ind., vol. 5, p. 498, 1891.

The red and common white rices are two separate and distinct strains. The seed of one will not produce the other. They are as distinct and as different as dent and sweet corn.

The white rice has been cultivated so long that it requires improved conditions to reach its best and fullest development.

Red rice is still practically a wild variety. It is a stronger and hardier grower, which will ripen its seed under more adverse conditions than the white rice. When the two are cross fertilized the red rice shows greater potency. The crosses show a preponderance of red "blood."

POSITION AS A WEED.

Professor Dodson, of the Louisiana Agricultural Experiment Station, discusses its relations to white-rice culture as follows:[1]

The popular idea that red rice comes up very early in the spring is in accordance with the facts as observed. Cultivation just before sowing, to kill the young plants, is productive of some good, but there are still grains of red rice in the ground that have not germinated, and some will not come up till quite late in the spring, after the white rice is rapidly growing. This is not only shown by direct experiment in tagging bunches of rice, but by the fact that one can go into the field almost at any period from the harvest to frost and find plants that are just maturing their first seed. It is to be noted that reference is made only to the stems from the original stooling, and the expression is not to be confounded with the second crop of seeds from suckers or branches of the stems after the tops have been cut off.

PERSISTENCE.

It is asserted by some planters that the seeds can remain in the soil for one or more years and then grow; that it requires more than one year to exterminate the red rice by cultivation. This subject has not been satisfactorily demonstrated, however, and it is possible that they are mistaken. Notwithstanding their honest protest that no plants were allowed to mature seed, it is possible that some plants ripened seed that escaped their observation. We have not been able to keep any seeds all summer in a moist soil. They either germinate or decay when the warm weather comes. But this is not the most important question, as we know that it can be soon exterminated from a field by thorough cultivation. The most important question is to prevent reseeding. After the crop is harvested, and there is generally but one harvest in the year, the stems that are cut often send out suckers of branches from the lower nodes, many of which will mature seeds before winter. This mode of reproduction takes place with the red rice as well as the white, but not to a greater extent, so there would be no greater proportional increase in the number of seeds, but as the winter approaches a remarkable difference in the provision for the winter preservation of seeds is exhibited.

From long cultivation the white rice has largely lost its power of self-preservation, and a little warm weather after the seed has matured will cause a large per cent to germinate if sufficient moisture is available. If they are on the ground, the fall rains, with the warm days that generally come in November and the early part of December, cause the seeds to germinate, and then they are killed by the winter cold. On the other hand, under the same conditions as above stated, hardly a grain of the red rice can be found that shows any evidence of germination. It is a law of nature that when a plant develops some character that makes it better suited

[1] Louisiana Agric. Exp. Sta. Bul. 50, p. 215.

to its surroundings, that character is apt to be maintained and developed in the off-spring of that plant; but if the character is of no service to the plant, it is likely to be lost. Again, if a character is once acquired and the surroundings become changed so that the character is not brought into service for many generations, the character is apt to be lost. As the white rice is carefully harvested and stored in a dry place over winter, it would have a tendency to lose the power that it once had of resisting the exposure to winter cold, while the red rice would retain the power to remain over winter without protection. In the following spring, of the seeds that had remained on the field, a large percentage of the red rice would grow, but only a small percentage of the white rice. It is not hard to understand why the idea should become prevalent that all the seeds that develop were of the red variety, or that the white seeds had developed plants that bore red seeds.

But the red-rice seeds are not alone dependent upon their power to resist premature-germination or decay, but a more remarkable character is exhibited in preventing the seed from being subjected to the moisture of the soil too soon. As will presently be explained, the red seeds are more apt than the white seeds to be preserved in a dry condition, and this character as much as any other will account for the greater increase in the number of seeds. The white stems generally decay at the nodes in the late fall or early winter, the upper part of the stem becomes separated from the lower, and the head of seeds falls to the ground. The stems of the red rice do not decay so readily at the nodes, but as the straw becomes overripe it weakens just above the first node below the head, or sometimes in the second internode, and the head falls over and remains hanging in this position. Many of the seeds become shattered off by the rain, by birds, and by the wind, but many are preserved in this way in a dry state till all danger of fall germination is averted. In going over the fields in winter it is not a difficult matter to find the red rice, owing to this tendency of the heads to remain attached and suspended, rendering them more conspicuous.

Again, some of the seeds that have not begun to grow at the spring plowing will be covered to a considerable depth, and of these many will fail to grow, but some of them will succeed in getting their little stems to the top of the ground, and it may be that the late plants are accounted for in this way.

In visiting the fields from time to time after the harvest one can find red rice in all stages of development. Most planters will state that the red rice matures a little in advance of the general crop of white rice, and this is true with many individual bunches, which may possibly be due to the fact that the seeds that have remained in the field all winter are in condition to germinate in advance of the planted rice. In every field visited just before or during harvest red rice was found that was riper than the general crop, but at the same time other plants were found that were not so ripe, varying from one to three weeks later in maturity, with a still smaller quantity that was much later.

This fact has possibly escaped the attention of the planter, because the difference in the appearance of the two heads is not very conspicuous till they are fully expanded, and after the general harvest close attention has not been given to the matter. * " *

After the red rice is once introduced into the field we can account for its increase, and the only reasonable explanation of its origin in the fields is that it was introduced there in impure seed.

REMEDY FOR RED RICE.

Two things must be accomplished to keep the fields clear of red rice:

First. Seed planted must be free of red rice, and the utmost caution must be exercised to secure this.

Second. Red seed must be prevented from maturing in the field if accidentally planted.

To this end it is exceedingly important to prevent a second crop of red seed from maturing after the general harvest, which is almost certain to occur if the field is left fallow till the following winter. The land should be well drained at the time of the harvest, and within a few weeks thereafter the stubble should be plowed under. In October thoroughly cultivate the land with the disk harrow and sow to oats for winter pasture. If the harvest be early, the stubble may be plowed under immediately and the field planted to vetches or crimson clover for pasture. It is a sound principle in agriculture that the land should be kept shaded as much as possible by some crop to be turned under if not required for pasture or for harvest. In pasturage, care should be exercised not to allow any stock on these fields in wet weather. Some have advised winter pasturing of rice fields with hogs. While they would be of some advantage in gleaning the land and preventing reseeding with late-maturing rice, this would be generally counterbalanced by the injury to levees and drains and is by no means a thorough method. Fall plowing and planting to forage crops is far more advantageous. It is quite customary to burn the stubble. This may destroy a few seeds and prevent sprouts from maturing seed, but it destroys fertilizers and leaves the land bare. Plowing in the early spring and thorough cultivation just before planting is helpful in reducing the red rice, but not sufficient for complete eradication.

On new land, seed absolutely free from red rice should be used; then, with care, the land may be kept free from it. In case land is already filled with it, if sufficiently well drained, cultivate to corn or cotton a few years; if not sufficiently well drained, summer fallow; if this can not be done, pasture to sheep or hogs. Every rice planter should use great care, in selecting a new piece of ground upon which to raise seed, to choose a plot without possible taint of red. The seed should be examined so closely as to prevent the sowing of any red seed.

RICE IN ASIA AND THE PACIFIC ISLANDS.

HAWAIIAN ISLANDS.

The islands of the Hawaiian group contain 6,740 square miles of territory, about sixth-sevenths the area of New Jersey. Like most volcanic islands they are mountainous and have comparatively small tracts of arable land suitable for coffee, sugar, rice, and other products. It is estimated that 6,915 acres are devoted to coffee, 125,000 acres to sugar, and 4,700 to rice. The rice lands are mostly low tracts along the coast, and are cultivated by Chinese.

The following statement concerning rice cultivation in the Hawaiian Islands is of interest:[1]

At the present time rice occupies the second place in the area of production and in the value of product. The total production can not be exactly estimated, since

---

[1] The Hawaiian Islands, by Walter Maxwell; Yearbook U. S. Department of Agriculture, 1898, p. 567.

a part is consumed upon the island. The exports of rice for 1897 were 5,499,499 pounds, valued at $225,575.52. The home consumption is large and would greatly augment the production indicated by the exports.

The lands used for rice are chiefly the lowest flats found at the outlets of valleys and close to the sea. These lands are generally fertile, but often too low and swampy for cane culture. These locations are favored with an abundance of sweet water, which is discharged into the sea, and this is a first essential condition in rice culture. During the growth of the crop, and up to the time of maturity, the lands bearing rice are held under water, which is kept gradually flowing and not allowed to stagnate and sour on the land.

The rice growers are almost wholly Chinamen. This race is able to work and thrive in conditions of location and climate which other peoples do not appear able to endure. From lowland climatic action, which is liable to induce low fevers, especially among the Japanese, the Chinaman is apparently immune. Certain small areas of low bog land in and about the suburbs of Honolulu are being rapidly drained, cultivated, and planted with vegetables or fruits, or overflowed with sweet running water to support the rice crop. The area of rice lands is not appreciably increasing. There is a tendency to use certain of these lands, which allow of it, for sugar growing, the present prices of sugar being very tempting.

THE PHILIPPINES.

Climatic conditions.—In the Philippine Islands rice culture varies considerably from the oriental type. There is very little hand cultivation of the soil. Plowing with the water buffalo is universal, with plows of the most primitive kind; sowing in beds and transplanting to the fields is the general rule, but there is considerable broadcast sowing in the fields. Climatic conditions have determined these variations from the general type. The rainy season commences in May. There is usually enough rain in this month to moisten the soil and fit it for plowing. In June or July the rice can be transplanted or sown in the fields, with a reasonable prospect that there will be sufficient rain to induce growth. In case of transplanting, the rice is sown in seed beds the same as in Japan or China. In some cases the tops of the young plants are pruned slightly. The plants are transplanted the latter part of July. In May or June, when the soil is moist, the fields are plowed; later the rains convert the plowed fields into shallow ponds, all outlets in the embankments surrounding them having been closed after plowing. The soil is then worked with a heavy rake, which converts the pond into mud; into this mud and water the rice plants are set. The heavy rains of July, August, and September flood the fields and perfect the crop.

The report of the observatory at Manila from 1880 to 1896, inclusive, shows the following average number of days in each month on which rain fell:

Month.	No. of days.	Inches of rainfall.[1]	Month.	No. of days.	Inches of rainfall.
January	4.3	1.15	August	19.8	13.08
February	2.2	.47	September	20.7	15.02
March	3.4	.65	October	14.4	7.47
April	3.5	1.11	November	11.3	4.92
May	9.2	4.2	December	8.4	2.09
June	15.4	9.68			
July	22.1	14.72	Total	134.7	74.56

[1] The rainfall is the average from 1865 to 1896, inclusive.

The annual rainfall ranges from 6½ to 10.1 feet, mostly falling in the months of June, July, August, September, and October. Under such conditions it requires very little assistance from the surrounding country to flood the rice fields. The direct rainfall. if retained by levees, is usually sufficient. This presents such favorable conditions that little has been done to secure systematic irrigation from rivers and mountain streams; yet irrigation would more than double the crop, because under the climatic conditions in these islands two crops of rice could be secured annually. The following table, compiled from the reports of the observatory at Manila, shows the mean temperature of each month for seventeen years ended 1897:

Month.	Degrees F.	Month.	Degrees F.
January	77	August	80.9
February	77.9	September	80.6
March	80.6	October	80.4
April	82.9	November	79
May	83.8	December	77.3
June	82.4		
July	80.0	Average	80.3

The average temperature is thus shown to be very favorable for the production of rice during the entire year. Under the system of agriculture in operation on these islands other farm products have been found more profitable than rice, and instead of being large exporters of this cereal they are considerable importers. The annual average of imports from 1886 to 1890 was 157,332,654 pounds.

Harvesting and yield.—The harvest occurs in December. The rice is cut, bound in very small bundles, and left upon the field until partially dry; it is then carried to the narrow levees around the field, and piled on top of them in long ricks about 2 feet high and as long as required for the amount of grain. The heads of the lower half of the rick are all in one direction, and hang over and clear of the bank; the heads of the upper half are in the reverse direction, and hang over and clear the butts of the straw of the lower section. It is thrashed by hand, dried on mats, and cleaned by winnowing. The average product per acre in the Philippines, under their tenant system, is about 600 pounds when no special attention is paid to irrigation. The largest estate in the islands gave me, from their books, the yield at 560 pounds of paddy per acre. On irrigated land the yield was 2,000 pounds. One man and a buffalo farms 2½ acres of rice; two men and four buffaloes farm 2½ acres of sugar cane. This shows that one man in the United States, with our improved machinery, is equal in the rice field to at least 30 Filipinos. They are paid for farm work 20 cents per day in silver, which is equal to 10 cents in gold, consequently their wages, while seemingly low, are as high, when compared with their earning capacity, as $3 per day for American farm hands. From the $3 per day, however, must be deducted, for a full comparison, the rental of the machinery.

The outlook for the future of rice cultivation in the Philippines is bright. The lands suitable for rice cultivation are of considerable extent. It ought to be only a matter of a dozen years or less for enterprising Americans to turn the tide from an annual importation of 150,000,000 pounds to a considerable export. There is already a large market for the product. It is the cheapest and most common food of oriental peoples, and following a peaceful settlement of the difficulties there, there will undoubtedly be a steady increase in the home demand for this product. What is wanted is such an application of modern methods to rice growing in the Philippines as the natural conditions there may admit.

JAPAN.

Rice forms the principal article of food of the Japanese, and its cultivation presents many interesting problems. First, about 43,000,000 of people must be sustained largely by the product of 7,000,000 acres of rice. This allows over 6 persons to the acre, and on the basis of the crop of 1896 furnishes $4\frac{1}{2}$ bushels of hulled rice for each person—about 150 pounds of milled rice. This indicates that Japan has attained a density of population which allows only a narrow margin between home consumption and possible production.

ACREAGE AND YIELD OF FOOD CROPS.

It must not, however, be inferred that rice is the sole food of the people. The daily ration includes a variety of foods of a highly nitrogenous character, which with vegetables supplement the rice. The following official report of the number of acres of food products produced annually in Japan will correct to some extent the impression that the Japanese subsist almost solely on rice:

Food crops of Japan as reported for 1896

Food crops.	Acres.	Total product, in bushels.	Product per acre, in bushels.
Rice [1]	6, 967, 461	180, 998, 855	26
Wheat	1, 104, 200	17, 763. 945	16. 09
Rye	1, 681, 267	14, 608, 117	8. 7
Barley	1, 626, 260	39, 246, 425	24. 1
Peas and beans	1, 343, 191	18, 063, 070	13. 4
Millet			
Buckwheat	2, 077, 982	28, 002, 330	10. 6
Rape			
Irish potatoes	57, 790	6, 862, 469	118. 75
Sweet potatoes	195, 251	68, 402, 579	350. 33

[1] The rice product is with hulls removed, and to compare with paddy about 20 per cent should be added.

The acreage devoted to rice can not be very much increased in Japan. The islands are of volcanic formation, and in a general way it may be stated that a rather bold range of mountains traverses the islands from the southwest to the northeast, occupying seven-eighths of the territory. The remaining one-eighth consists of fertile valleys, widening toward the sea until they gradually expand into coastal deltas of considerable extent. The narrow valleys are terraced on each side; at the base of the mountains canals are made to receive the descending rivulets and convey the water to the various fields as required for irrigation. Frequently the surplus water is used to turn an overshot wheel for milling rice or for manufacturing purposes in the native villages or it may be allowed to flow into some creek or river; but as far as possible sufficient mountain water for irrigation is conducted by canals at a level somewhat higher than the rice fields. The ingenuity displayed in devising the elaborate system of irrigating canals in Japan and the amount of patient industry required to construct them are simply marvelous. The extent of the retaining walls constructed to prevent the washing of the terraces, or to arrest mountain slides, or as barriers against a river bent on destroying a field is inconceivable. These are the works of a patient and industrious people through many years. Occasionally water for irrigation is elevated from a creek or river, but almost invariably by the simplest machinery, such as has been employed for hundreds of years.

METHODS OF CULTURE.

Rice production in all oriental countries is conducted upon the same general plan, but the methods differ so materially from those employed in the United States that they should be carefully noted. The lands are divided by levees into small fields, many of them not more than a few square rods in area, and seldom containing more than half an acre. They are of no regular form, and generally the inclosing levees are gracefully curved to represent some ideal of beauty in the mind of the planter. In the small valleys among the mountains these curved embankments were doubtless necessary to conform to the mountains and inclose a larger area, but as the improvements encroached upon the low lands curves continued to be used. These fields are well drained and thoroughly worked, mostly by hand. In traveling a hundred miles through rice sections where the fields were being prepared for the crop, possibly in two or three cases an ox may be seen used for plowing—otherwise men are turning the soil with mattock or spade. Both of these implements differ from those used in the United States. The mattock has a blade about 16 inches long and 5 inches wide, with a handle 4 or 5 feet long. The implement weighs 7 or 8 pounds. With a quick, powerful blow this is buried into the soil about 14 inches, then, using the handle as a lever, the soil is disintegrated and partially inverted. The spade is a wooden blade about 2 feet long with an ordinary handle; the lower end of the blade is cased with steel, and upon the back of the upper end is a block the width of the spade. The spade is thrust into the soil by the foot at an angle of about 30°, and, using the block for a fulcrum, the soil is rolled to one side as in plowing, only that it is more thoroughly disintegrated. All the trash, straw, or grass upon the field is turned under, together with such an amount of lime, ashes, fish manure, or human excreta as the farmer may be able to procure. Where a winter crop is raised the manure is generally applied in the fall. If the rice field remains fallow during the winter the manure is applied at the time of spring working in March or April, according to conditions. The seed bed is prepared as early as convenient in the spring, and thoroughly manured. It is then spaded 8 inches deep and worked till the manure is thoroughly incorporated and all clods pulverized. It is prepared with the care of a bed in a garden. It is then surrounded by a low ridge and water admitted to fill the soil until the spaded earth becomes consistent mud. The seed, which had been previously selected for purity, size of grain, and flinty character, is then soaked in pure water till well sprouted, which usually requires two days, and sown on the bed broadcast as thickly as admissible for strong plants. Prior to sowing, the bed is covered with water to the depth of 2½ inches. In five or six days the rice is well started. It is then left dry in the daytime and is flooded at night. Covering with water at night keeps it warm, and allowing the bed to be dry in the daytime admits air and prevents sun scalding, which frequently occurs when the rice is young and the covering of water is shallow.

Early in June, when the rice is 8 or 10 inches high, it is pulled up, tied in bundles of six to ten plants, and transplanted into the fields. The fields have been prepared and flooded to the depth of 1½ to 4 inches. The rice plants are set in rows about 1 foot apart and at a distance of 10 to 12 inches in the row, on the richest lands, making 9 bunches to the yard. On poor lands double that number might be set. They are set so that the soil covers the root. Thereafter the flow of water is not continuous. In a few days it is drawn off, and an application of rape seed, oil cake, or fish scraps is made to the surface. As soon as the fertilizer has had time to become incorporated with the soil, water is again applied and withdrawn, for the crop to be hoed. Every weed is cut out, and in some cases the roots are slightly pruned. Each field is given the minute attention of a garden. When the growing period is well advanced the water is allowed to remain permanently upon the field, care being taken to renew it by gentle inflow and escape. The water is allowed to remain till a slight change in color indicates that the period of ripening is approaching. It is then withdrawn. While the slight change of color is given as the guide, the time when the milk in the seed has become dough is more correct; for the Japanese cut their rice when the straw is scarcely turned. Both the straw and the rice are better when the harvest occurs before the grain is dead ripe.

CUTTING.

The grain is cut close to the earth with a small sickle-like knife set in a handle. Four hills or bunches are bound together with two straws, making a bundle 3 or 4 inches in diameter. These are generally laid crosswise in small piles, and are allowed to dry during the day. At evening they are hung on bamboo poles, with heads down. Two bamboo poles are made into a structure like a fence by means of cross sticks. The lower pole is high enough so that the heads of the suspended bundles come within about a foot of the ground. The upper pole is 18 to 20 inches above this, the rice bundles on the upper pole overlapping the bundles below. After the bundles hang upon the poles long enough to become dry, they are taken down by women, and the grain removed by drawing the heads through a hetchel. The grain is then placed upon mats and exposed to the sun till thoroughly dry. Before it is sent to market the hulls are removed by passing the grain through a pair of burs made of cement and bamboo and worked by hand. Winnowing is done by the open-air process, or by a simple fanning mill.

The milled product is then placed in sacks deftly made of rice straw, each holding about 133⅓ pounds, in which it is transported to market. This rice sack is afterwards sold for paper material.

UPLAND RICE.

Considerable is said from time to time about upland rice, and many applications have been made for seed. Rice is a plant of such a wide range of adaptation that most of its varieties will thrive on well-cultivated, fertile, high land. The plant under such conditions appears, in favorable seasons, to grow about as well as in a marsh. In former years it was frequently planted in the cotton rows. The grain product of such rice is always uncertain, and never satisfactory. It seldom yields more than one-third the amount produced on an equal area of irrigated land, 550 pounds per acre under dry cultivation corresponding to 2,000 pounds under irrigation, and the grain is of an inferior quality. Very little rice is produced in Japan by dry cultivation. Professor Chamberlain, an authority on things Japanese, states that all high-class rice requires flooding, only an inferior sort being grown in the dry. It is hardly wise to encourage in the United States a cultivation which is only adopted as a matter of necessity in countries of such density of population that consumption and possible production are about equal.

MANURE.

The extent to which night soil is used for fertilizing soils is scarcely conceivable. Whether in city or country it is practically all saved in earthen receptacles and removed once or twice daily, according to the weather. This is carried in wooden buckets balanced on a pole across the shoulder. In cities the collectors sell to fertilizer companies what a man can carry (about 40 gallons) for 10 cents in silver. The companies transport it on flatboats to the rural districts, where it is applied in the liquid form. In one corner of almost every garden and field may be found a cistern for storing liquid manure.

While Japan is a small country there is considerable variation in climate, due to the warm ocean current striking the southeastern coast of Kiushu. In the central provinces much of the rice is not cut until well into November. A traveler passing over the railroad from Tokyo to Kobe on November 8, 1898, stated that at that time not one-half of the rice was harvested. The best rice is produced in the island of Kiushu. The fields are larger, more attention is paid to the seed, the climate is better suited to the rice crop, and the annual product per acre is larger. Special attention is called to the large percentage of fats in Japan rice, indicative of high flavor.

ABSENCE OF LABOR-SAVING MACHINERY.

The introduction of modern labor saving machinery in rice production in Japan is practically impossible. There are few horses or oxen in the rural districts, and there is not sufficient food to keep any considerable number without drawing from what is absolutely necessary for the subsistence of the people. There is labor enough to cultivate all the soil under the present methods, and if machinery were introduced that labor would be idle. It requires the most intensive cultivation of the soil to produce an adequate supply of food. Machinery would be less thorough than the present methods. The roads to the fields are so narrow that in most cases machinery like the harvester and binder could not traverse them. The fields are so small, and frequently their boundaries are so tortuous, that the plow could not be used to advantage. In the island of Yezo the population is less dense, and American machinery has been introduced to some extent.

Common laborers on the farm in Japan receive on an average 6 cents (gold) per day for women and 10 cents for men, with board, except in harvest time, when they are paid about double. It is doubtful whether plowing has any advantage over spading at such rate of wages. It is difficult to see how there could be any change in the methods of planting. The present system of transplanting insures the best results, and allows time to take off the winter crop.

Harvesting in Japan is expensive, considering the price of labor. On the 9th of November, 1898, when returning from a visit to the Kinkakuji Gardens in Kioto, I passed through a rice field where two laborers were cutting. They stated that they were paid two yen ($1 gold) for cutting, binding, and hanging on poles the rice in a small field by the roadside. On measuring it there was found to be two-elevenths of an acre. This was at the rate of $5.50 (gold) per acre. By the hand processes the straw, which is quite valuable, is preserved, the grain is cut at the right time, even where there is a variation of maturity in the same field, and there is no loss from the cracking of the kernels by the hetchel.

Rice among the farmers of Japan is considered quite a luxury and many can not afford to eat it regularly. It is eaten by such only on certain days or in case of sickness. Professor Chamberlain says in his book, Things Japanese:

We once heard a beldame in a country village remark to another, with a grave shake of the head, "What! do you mean to say that it has come to having to give her rice?"—the unexpressed inference being that the patient's case must be alarming indeed if the family had thought it necessary to resort to so expensive a dainty.

Among the poorer farmers barley, millet, and sweet potatoes are substituted for rice. Mr. Shiraishi, a silk manufacturer of Omata, is noted for the kind treatment of his operatives. The bill of fare in his boarding house consists of boiled rice, boiled rape and *daikon* (half radish and half turnip), bean soup, and barley tea for breakfast and dinner; lunch at noon is the same without the bean soup. In the higher schools board consists of boiled rice, a soup made from dried fish, two kinds of vegetables, and tea, with bean soup for one meal daily.

INDIA.

The population of India, including Burmah, is placed at about 287,200,000 on a total area of 1,800,258 square miles, about half the area of the United States. Rice forms the principal food of this great number of people. Nearly 60,000,000 acres are devoted to this cereal. Rice has been under cultivation so many centuries and under such a great diversity of conditions that many varieties, numbering into the hundreds, have resulted. These varieties range from those which thrive in salt or brackish marshes along the coast and require a long hot season to attain maturity to types maturing on the mountain slopes of northern India at elevations of from 7,000 to 10,000 feet. Some varieties grow only in deep water, others are dry-land forms cultivated in the cotton rows or in fields where no water is obtainable for irrigation. The greatest variations occur in methods of seeding, cultivation, and harvesting, and there are equally great differences in the yield, quality, and value of the crop. The methods are, in the main, similar to those used in Japan. Modern machinery is not used to any appreciable extent for the same reasons that prevail in Japan. India, the British Straits Settlements, and Hongkong export large quantities of rice, much of which finally reaches the American market here and in the Philippines.

CHINA.

China has more land adapted to the production of rice than any other country of equal extent. From the southern boundary to the Yellow River and from the China Sea far into the interior it is mainly a vast network of canals and rice fields. The industry of the Chinese has made these remarkably productive and capable of sustaining an exceedingly dense population.

The methods of rice production in China are so nearly like those of Japan that they do not require special description, and the full statement made about Japan can stand as a type of oriental countries, noting the important differences that may exist. The Chinese have not the elaborate irrigation of Japan. Much more pumping is done, but by the most primitive methods, such as were used in Egypt two thousand years ago. The plow is in more common use than in Japan. That used is a crude affair made of wood, shod with iron, yet the patient Chinaman manages to do fairly good work with it, though he seldom stirs the soil deeper than 4 inches. The other implements of tillage are the spade and the hoe, both of a primitive sort.

The rice is planted in beds and transplanted in the same way as in Japan. Harvesting is practically the same, except that the bundles are not usually placed on bamboo poles for drying, but are dried in small piles. Thrashing is done with the flail, or by the trampling of oxen. The rice is mainly sent to market in the paddy. Fertilizers are used as far as it is practicable to secure them. In the interior districts, where it is impossible to irrigate, upland rice is planted. This is not transplanted. The seed is sown in drills upon well-manured soil and carefully cultivated. Centuries of production under such conditions have undoubtedly resulted in varieties better suited to upland conditions than ordinary rice. The yield per acre is so much less than for irrigated rice that it is an unprofitable crop where irrigation is possible. For upland culture, wheat and oats are more profitable than rice where they can be grown. China has so many navigable rivers and canals that the principal interior commerce of the country, including the rice crop, is carried by water.

OTHER COUNTRIES OF ASIA.

Rice is an important factor in the commerce of almost all oriental countries.

SIAM.

Since the repeal of the law (1856) forbidding the exportation of rice till a three years' supply was stored for home consumption, the rice industry in Siam has received a great impetus. Vast areas of rich virgin soil have been brought under cultivation and planted to rice. These coast plains are crossed by canals for irrigation and the transportation of their products. The canals were easily constructed, and have from rivers an ample supply of fresh water. Two crops are produced annually. Many Chinese have settled in Siam and engaged in the production of rice. With the increase in capital a large gain in production may be expected and Siam will become quite a factor in the world's supply. There is an abundance of labor. The rice fields include about one-third of an acre, surrounded by low banks of earth. Planting for the main crop commences in June, when the rains have inundated the fields; transplanting is the usual course. This is the commercial crop, and is harvested in October. Rice sown later is harvested in January or February. Implements are exceedingly primitive. Cutting, thrashing, and cleaning are by the same methods followed in China.

At Bangkok there were in October, 1890, 23 steam rice mills using modern machinery. The first steam mill in Siam was established by an American who, not finding it profitable, abandoned the enterprise, but the business has since become exceedingly important, and new mills are constantly in construction. In 1888 eight new mills were erected by Chinese owners and two by English. The Chinese employ the best European engineers, and many of the mills are lighted by electricity and have double gangs of workmen, thus running day and night. The fuel used in these mills consists entirely of rice husks, consumed in furnaces especially built for the purpose. Five of the mills at Bangkok produce thoroughly cleaned rice, but most of the mills only perform a partial cleaning, leaving 20 per cent of paddy in the rice, with which it is said to keep better when shipped than if every grain were cleaned.[1]

COCHIN CHINA, ANAM, AND TONQUIN.

In proportion to population Cochin China produces a large amount of rice for export, and is able to supply the shortage of a number of countries. The reports of export from Saigon, the capital, show that rice is an important factor in the commerce of the port. The total production has been reported as high as 1,200,000,000 pounds, of which 800,000,000 are exported. This is doubtless an overstatement, as it would require that nearly every acre be devoted to rice to yield so large an annual crop.

Anam is also a large producer of rice, but not to the extent of the consumption.

The lowlands of Tonquin are almost exclusively devoted to rice; but the population is so dense that the production is only equal to the consumption. Rice is mainly raised by irrigation, and yields two crops per annum.

PERSIA AND ASIA MINOR.

Rice is extensively cultivated in Persia and thrives even upon the higher plateaus, but not as well as in the lowlands near the coast. In the main it is produced only for home consumption and hence does not affect the markets of the world. The usual Asiatic methods are employed in production. Very little rice is grown in Asia Minor, Egyptian rice being chiefly imported for the home consumption.

---

[1] Information partly from consular report No. 95, July, 1888.

RICE IN AFRICA.

Egypt is the principal rice-producing country in Africa. The rich Nile delta is admirably adapted to its cultivation. The rice is sown while the lands are still covered with water in the annual inundation, and is generally scattered broadcast. It germinates in a few days, the rich deposits of silt from the overflow provide favorable conditions for growth, and the crop makes profitable returns. The annual product is more than sufficient for home consumption. The surplus goes to Turkey. Rice is grown also in many other portions of Africa to some extent, particularly in the French colonies, but only for home use.

Madagascar produces some rice and supplies to a certain extent her local market. Africa, as a whole, is not as well adapted to rice as Asia—too large a portion of the country is high table-land.

RICE IN EUROPE.

Italy is the only country in Europe that produces more rice than sufficient to meet the demands of home consumption. The method of cultivation is similar to that pursued in South Carolina. The cultivation is thorough and the industry profitable.

Spain has grown more or less rice since the time of the Moorish conquest. About 1860 a portion of the delta of Ebro was placed under irrigation by an elaborate system of canals, and rice was planted with such success that lands rose in value rapidly, in some cases increasing fifty-fold. Other portions of Spain produce rice to some extent.

RICE IN CENTRAL AND SOUTH AMERICA.

Some of the smaller States of Central America produce considerable rice of excellent quality. The planters of Louisiana have for some years obtained an excellent variety of rice seed from Honduras. It stands up well. The stalk is stiff and resists the wind. The head is large and the grains of good size and flinty.

In South America rice does not appear to have been grown as a staple crop, though a considerable amount has been raised in some States. Many of the conditions appear to be favorable for the future development of this industry. In the United States of Colombia there is a large consumption of rice per capita, but it is mainly imported.

www.ingramcontent.com/pod-product-compliance
Lightning Source LLC
Chambersburg PA
CBHW022029080426
42733CB00007B/779